W9-CEO-740

FOLKLORE IN AMERICA

TRISTRAM P. COFFIN, who was born in San Marino, California, and grew up in Rhode Island, attended Haverford College, the University of Virginia, and the University of Pennsylvania, from which he received a doctorate in 1949. He is professor of English and vice-dean of the Graduate School of Arts and Sciences at the University of Pennsylvania. He has been Secretary-Treasurer of the American Folklore Society (1961–65). A 1953 Guggenheim Fellow, Mr. Coffin has lectured widely and conducted courses in folklore and folksong for commercial and educational television. His published work includes numerous articles on balladry, his special interest. Among his books are *The British Traditional Ballad in North America, The Critics and the Ballad* (edited with MacEdward Leach) and *Indian Tales of North America.*

HENNIG COHEN was born in Darlington, South Carolina, and studied at the University of South Carolina. After service in the Air Force during World War II, he received his Ph.D. in 1951 from Tulane University. Now professor of English at the University of Pennsylvania, Mr. Cohen was a Guggenheim Fellow in 1960. He is the former executive secretary of the American Studies Association (1956–61) and since 1958 has edited the *American Quarterly.* In addition to articles on American literature, history, and folklore, Mr. Cohen has written *The South Carolina Gazette, 1732–1775* and edited *The Battle-Pieces of Herman Melville* and *Selected Poems of Herman Melville* (Anchor A375). He is co-editor of the Anchor Documents in American Civilization series.

FOLKLORE IN AMERICA

TALES, SONGS, SUPERSTITIONS,

PROVERBS, RIDDLES, GAMES,

FOLK DRAMA AND FOLK FESTIVALS

Selected and Edited by
Tristram P. Coffin and Hennig Cohen
from the *Journal of American Folklore*

ANCHOR BOOKS
DOUBLEDAY & COMPANY, INC.
GARDEN CITY, NEW YORK

All of the selections in this volume are from the *Journal of American Folklore* and are reprinted with the permission of the American Folklore Society.

Folklore in America was originally published in a hardbound edition by Doubleday & Company, Inc. in 1966.

Anchor Books edition: 1970

Copyright © 1966 by Tristram P. Coffin and Hennig Cohen
All Rights Reserved
Printed in the United States of America

For MacEdward Leach

CONTENTS

Introduction   xiii

The Folktale   1

Turtle Surpasses Man in Ingenuity
   (West African)   3
Saru-to-kani (Japanese)   3
Adam and Eve and Their Children
   (Isleta Pueblo Indian)   4
The Bear Husband (Armenian)   5
Min Tzŭ Chien (Chinese)   7
Les Cartes du Nommé Richard
   (French Canadian)   9
The Priestwife Gets a Beating (Greek)   11
The King and Old George Buchanan (Scottish)   12
Dividing the Chicken (Irish)   14
An Alsatian Witch Story (German)   14
Why the Irish Came to America
   (Irish-American)   15
Brer Rabbit's Cool Air Swing (American Negro)   17
Valpariso and Lily White (Dutch-American)   19
The Flute Player (Micmac Indian-Negro)   23
The Mean Rich Man (Spanish-American)   25
Wait Till Emmett Comes (American Negro)   26
The Man Who Plucked the Corberie
   (Anglo-American)   28
Big Lies from Grassy (Anglo-American)   29
A Numskull Story (Anglo-American)   32
The Preacher and the Hog (Anglo-American)   33
Rip Van Winkle (Spanish-American)   34
Juan José (Puerto Rican)   34

The Fire-Hunt (Anglo-American)   36
Shakespeare's Ghost (Anglo-American)   37
Stories about Mr. Mac (Anglo-American)   38
How the Town Was Named Elkader
    (Anglo-American)   41
Night Doctors (American Negro)   42
The Soldier Who Used His Head
    (Anglo-American)   43
The Three Chaplains Play Cards (Jewish)   44
Using the Telephone (Cornish-American)   44

THE FOLKSONG   47

The Two Sisters (Anglo-American)   49
An Indian Love Song (Sioux Indian)   51
La Randonnée de la Ville de Paris
    (French Canadian)   53
Trippa, Troppa, Tronjes (Dutch-American)   55
Songs for Christmas and the New Year
    (Cape Verde Negro)   56
The Ocean Burial (Anglo-American)   61
La Estrella del Norte (Spanish-American)   63
Ein Stevleik (Norwegian-American)   64
Ten Thousand Miles Away (Anglo-American)   68
Pig in the Parlor (Anglo-American)   70
I've a Long Time Heard (Anglo-American)   71
Ain't Gwine Grieve My God No More
    (American Negro)   72
Railroad Blues (American Negro)   74
Lob-Gesang (Amish)   75
The Death of the Beckwith Child
    (Anglo-American)   78
Asesinato de Francisco Villa (Spanish-American)   81
Silver Jack (Anglo-American)   85
I'm a Good Old Rebel (Anglo-American)   87
Bishop Zack (Mormon)   88
Sellin' That Stuff (American Negro)   89
McKinley and Huey Long (Anglo-American)   90

The Haunted Wood (Anglo-American) 93
Rhymes from Hawaii (Hawaiian-American) 95
The Dehorn Song (Anglo-American) 99

SUPERSTITIONS 101

To Charm Cattle and Cure Injuries (Finnish) 103
A Sponge Fishers' Charm (Greek) 105
Ogres: Dracos and Baboulas (Greek) 105
Omens of Death and Disaster (Japanese) 106
Dreams (Syrian) 107
Water Sleeps (Spanish-American) 109
Brujas in Texas (Spanish-American) 109
Witches Outwitted (German-American) 111
Will-o'-the-wisp (Louisiana French Negro) 113
Sign of a Hard Winter (Welsh-American) 113
Signs and Countersigns (American Negro) 114
Halloween Projects (Anglo-American) 115
Cross-marks (American Negro) 116
A Cross-mark to Relieve Distress
  (American Negro) 117
Aches and Pains (American Negro) 117
Warts (Creole) 119
Good Luck and Bad Luck (Anglo-American) 120
Spit and Sneeze (Creole) 122
Pins and Needles (Creole) 123
Beliefs about Marriage (Anglo-American) 124
Beliefs about Children (Anglo-American) 126
Hoodoo (Creole) 128
Flyting with Witches (Anglo-American) 131
To Foil a Witch (Anglo-American) 133
Plants, Birds, Animals and Insects
  (Anglo-American) 134
Nudity and Planting Customs (Anglo-American) 137

PROVERBS 141

Yiddish Proverbs (Russian-Jewish) 142
Coplas from New Mexico (Spanish-American) 145

Proverbs from Massachusetts (Anglo-American)   149
A Proverbial Rhyme (Anglo-American)   149
Gullah Proverbs (American Negro)   150
Geechee Proverbs (American Negro)   150

RIDDLES   153

Polish Riddles   154
Lithuanian Riddles   154
Syrian Riddles   156
Mexican Riddles   157
Pennsylvania Dutch Riddles   157
A Connecticut Riddle Tale (Anglo-American)   160
Riddles from South Carolina (American Negro)   160
Riddles from South Carolina, with Variants
    (American Negro)   161
Riddles from Louisiana (American Negro)   164
Riddles from New Jersey (American Negro)   165
Ozark Mountain Riddles (Anglo-American)   165
A Blue Ridge Mountain Riddle
    (Anglo-American)   167
Riddles from Tennessee (Anglo-American)   167
Riddles from Arkansas (Anglo-American)   169

GAMES   171

Woskate Takapsice or Sioux Shinney
    (Sioux Indian)   173
The King's Army (Anglo-American)   176
A Game with Eggs on Easter (Syrian)   177
A Counting Game (Portuguese Azores)   177
A Rapid Counting Contest (Mexican)   178
A Mexican Ring Game   179
The Little Coyote (Mexican)   179
A Guessing Game with Pecans
    (Louisiana French)   180
Club Fist (Pamunkey Indian)   180
Ring Games of Negro Children
    (American Negro)   181

Quebec Town (Anglo-American)   184
An Evening Party Song-Game
    (Anglo-American)   184
Snap (Anglo-American)   186
A Ball-Bouncing Game (Anglo-American)   187
A Ball-Bouncing and Rope-Jumping Song
    (Anglo-American)   188
Jump-Rope Rhymes (Anglo-American)   188
A Political Jump-Rope Rhyme (Anglo-American)   189
Counting Out Rhymes, with Variants
    (Anglo-American)   190
A Children's Dance Rhyme (Anglo-American)   191
Hop Scotch (Anglo-American)   192

FOLK DRAMA AND FOLK FESTIVAL   195

A Miracle Play of the Rio Grande
    (Spanish-American)   197
Christmas Masking in Boston (Anglo-American)   204
A Mummers' Play from the Kentucky Mountains
    (Anglo-American)   205
Seeking Jesus (American Negro)   211
Mother, Mother, the Milk's Boiling Over
    (Anglo-American)   212
A Ring Game from North Carolina
    (American Negro)   213
A Slovak Harvest Festival in New Jersey   214
A Corpus Christi Festival in Pennsylvania
    (German)   217
The *Penitentes* of New Mexico
    (Spanish-American)   220
A Lenten Procession in Arizona (Yaqui Indian)   224

NOTES ON SOURCES   227

INDEX   247

INTRODUCTION

A simple chart demonstrates the three traditions of literature which flourish in a country like ours.

1. Literary Tradition ⟶
2. Popular Tradition ⟶ } The Culture
3. Oral or Folk Tradition ⟶

Literary tradition represents the material written and read by persons of some education. This is what we study in the schools and colleges; and through it we receive and pass on to our children the bulk of our beliefs, ideals, and standards. Books like Herman Melville's *Moby-Dick,* stories like Mark Twain's *The Celebrated Jumping Frog of Calaveras County,* and poems like Henry Wadsworth Longfellow's *The Courtship of Miles Standish,* all lie along this line. Oral tradition is made up of the material that men and women who can't, don't, or won't write pass on from generation to generation by word of mouth. Among a primitive people like the pre-Columbian American Indians, all literature was oral; in a society like that of medieval Europe, a large portion of the literature was oral; but in a modern society like twentieth-century America, only a small portion of the literature (a few songs and tales, games and rhymes, jokes, proverbs, superstitions, and riddles) is transmitted directly from parent to child, without being recorded and disseminated through print and what we call the "mass media." Although some people may quibble, let's say that "literature flourishing in oral tradition is folklore,"[1] and hold to this definition.

[1] Many anthropologists distinguish between primitive literature (oral tradition that has had little contact with literary

Folklore cannot survive in a set form. Folklore continually changes, varying and developing, because it is shaped by the memories, creative talents, and immediate needs of human beings in particular situations. This process, the process of oral variation, is the lifeblood of folklore. When it is halted by printing or recording, folklore enters a state of suspended animation. It comes alive again only when it flows back into oral circulation.

Understanding the broad distinction between literary tradition and oral or folk tradition is simple enough: the one is written down, usually identified with an individual, and fixed in a preferred form; the other is transmitted by personal contact, tends to be anonymous, and changes so frequently that it has innumerable forms. It is popular tradition that is most troublesome. Wherever a nation has developed a literary tradition, it has also developed a popular tradition. In modern America, the popular tradition includes all sorts of promotional material, magazine and newspaper sub-literature, radio and television entertainment and the like, which is disseminated to huge groups of people through the mass media. The songs of Stephen Foster, George Gershwin, and Bob Dylan which deliberately imitate folk music because it is profitable to do so; the calculated promotion of fictional figures like Pecos Bill and Paul Bunyan in order to provide the local color that attracts tourists; the transformation by script writers of Billy the Kid and Davy Crockett into television heroes to sell cereal; and even the more or less innocent fabrication of children's stories such as that of George Washington and the cherry tree, designed to teach reading and moral behavior—fall within the popular tradition. It would be no problem to understand such material and to dismiss it as an inferior portion of the literary tradition, were it not for the fact that American entrepreneurs have

---

tradition) and folk literature (oral tradition that has been continually influenced by literary tradition). For our present purposes, we need not make this distinction.

learned that popular literature will sell better, do its job
better, if it imitates or disguises itself as folklore. As a
result, America has been and is now producing a mass of
sub-literary, popular material that masquerades as a product of oral tradition, even though the people who can't,
don't, or won't read know little of it and care less. For
instance, you can't collect Pecos Bill stories from real
cowhands, or Paul Bunyan stories from real loggers, or
"My Old Kentucky Home" from the folk, unless the person
you collect from has absorbed this popular lore through
sophisticated sources. Popularity in itself does not create
folklore.

Of course, it is difficult, even for the experts, to distinguish clearly between popular tradition and folk tradition,
just as it is difficult to decide whether or not Ibert's
Divertissement is a classical or "semi-classical" composition. Neatly drawn charts are seldom satisfactory. The
chart we have provided is even less so because the three
traditions (literary, popular, and oral or folk) freely ab-
sorb and exchange material. Authors like Joel Chandler
Harris and Washington Irving rewrite and reset well-
known folktales; singers within the oral tradition develop
folksongs from popular hits; and composers within the
popular tradition derive popular songs from folksongs.
Look at these instances. Dan Emmett, the minstrel, wrote
two songs, "I Wisht I Was In Dixie" and "Old Dan
Tucker." Both are known to millions of Americans. "Dixie"
is a popular song that has never entered folk tradition.
"Old Dan Tucker" was used as a play-party and square
dance song. Changed as it was used, it developed new
stanzas, and has been re-created so completely and so
often in oral transmission that it is now a genuine folksong. However, not long ago, a version of "Old Dan
Tucker" was being played by disc jockeys all across the
nation. One version, rewritten, had *re-entered* popular
tradition. A Negro woman who had composed a well-
known blues song from which she had collected royalties

for years appeared on a television show. She was amazed to find that the guitarist in the studio had learned her song from a folk informant in Louisiana, with a slightly different melody and radically different lyrics. Nor are these isolated cases. One picks up a book called *Folk Medicine*, which has nothing to do with cures known to the Vermont folk; he purchases a treasury of folklore that includes genuine folktales, anecdotes about popular heroes like Paul Bunyan, and even tales by a literary figure such as Mark Twain; he hears a radio announcer tell him baseball is the great American folk game. Naturally, he becomes confused. All too rightly, he realizes that he is not an expert, although he must be an expert if he is to know what folklore means or if he is to distinguish between the literary, the popular, and the folk traditions.

However, if he thinks he has difficulties when he is dealing with the word "folklore," he has only to talk about "*American* folklore" to compound them many times over. For in a culturally diverse nation like America, in a nation that came into being so recently and rapidly, it is risky to insist that a national folklore exists at all. There is, to be sure, a popular lore that is national in character and which is known to the nation as a whole, but this lore, featuring its Paul Bunyans, Johnny Appleseeds, and Pecos Bills, is largely the product of magazines and newspapers, Chambers of Commerce, television and motion picture studios, and professional patriots. The folk themselves learn almost nothing of such matter through oral tradition.

Historically, American folk groups have found their homogeneity arising from their occupational, regional, or ethnic identities. As the nation formed and nationalism began to replace localism, folk groups were being subjected to education and communication so intensively that they became sophisticated or sub-literary before they were able to develop a *national* homogeneity. Therefore, in America, one can find a vigorous oral tradition only where he finds a group that is isolated along occupational, regional, or ethnic lines. For example, one cannot collect much folklore from the Germans in New York State, because the Germans in New York have lost their ethnic identity through intermarriage and acculturation and because they have moved up the social and educational ladder. Such people are apt to know more about Paul Bunyan than they do about poltergeists. However, in Pennsylvania, where for religious reasons the Germans have maintained their isolation, one can still collect genuine German folklore, but will also find a certain indifference to America as a nation.

This means that a folklorist who attempts to treat American folklore as an entity is bold indeed. What he really has to do is to talk of ethnic, regional, or occupational lores in America. When the American Folklore Society was founded in 1888 its members followed lines of division that were essentially ethnic. The Society divided American folklore into these parts: (1) relics of British lore; (2) Negro lore; (3) American Indian lore; (4) lore of recent, unacculturated, ethnic groups (the French, the Spanish, the Swedes, and so forth). However, this is but an initial breakdown. Regional and occupational divisions exist along with the ethnic ones. Where a group of distinct racial and linguistic stock lives in a prolonged state of isolation, it may well develop regional characteristics that are more marked than its ethnic ones. This is the case, for example, with the British mountain whites, the Gullah Negroes of the coastal islands of Georgia and South Carolina, the Pennsylvania Dutch, and the Louisiana French. The same is true when the work of the group has led toward isolation over prolonged periods. Thus, Scotch-Irish lumbermen develop a different lore from Scotch-Irish sailors and Scotch-Irish rivermen. And so it goes with ethnic, occupational, and regional individualities fusing and re-forming at a rapid rate to create folk groups such as the Mormons of Utah, the Negroes of the northern American cities, the cowpunchers—groups whose identity results from a complex interplay of ethnic, regional, and

occupational factors that almost defies description. More-
over, all these folk groups are affected by their social and
economic positions, their levels of education, their religion, and their relationship to the mass media. What they
accept and reject, what their local attachments are, how
reliant they are on their particular practices and heritages
—such factors make it all but impossible to speak of
American folklore both as a unit and meaningfully.

Perhaps, the closest one comes to treating American
folklore as a unit is when he traces the life history of a
story or song that has been diffused widely in this country.
For example, the old tale, "The Deck of Cards," has found
its way into Maine, Michigan, and Pennsylvania lumber
camps, onto the frontier with the buffalo skinners, and
into the repertoire of all sorts of hill folk, cowboys, and
city people. Originally European, it has been shared all
over this country by men of French, African, British descent—becoming American as they have. "Been on the
Cholly So Long," a railroad hobo song with variants about
Jay Gould's daughter and a porter named Jimmy Jones,
was recast to fit the death of an Illinois Central engineer,
John Luther "Casey" Jones. It spread from the Midwest
across the nation. Adapted by a vaudeville team, it was
taken by American troops to Europe and Asia, rewritten
by labor agitators, and burlesqued by Mormons in a version called "Bishop Zack." But one has to remember that
for every song or superstition like these there are dozens of
accounts of local events and characters that never leave
the confines of the particular ethnic, occupational, or regional group that has spawned them out of its pride and
individuality. America may be the melting pot of the
world, but the fusions have generally taken place above
the level of folk culture, after the effects of education and
mass communication and acculturation have been felt.

Today, in a highly literate America, folklore is big business. Every year thousands of books, records, concerts,

and dramatic productions are created to satisfy the immense desire Americans have for a folk heritage.

In their eagerness to discover this heritage, most Americans have bothered little with such scholarly distinctions as those between popular lore and folklore. As long as the material is Americana, suggests the growth of democracy, and can in some way be ascribed to the masses or folks in general, the educated public has been willing to accept it as folklore. That much of it is bogus, has been created for quick commercial consumption, or is designed to inspire a political response seems to be of little matter. Parson Weems' George Washington, Longfellow's Priscilla Alden, even Walt Disney's Davy Crockett are not only allowed to stand side by side with genuine folk figures such as Mike Fink, John Henry, and Juan Bobo, but they frequently elbow them aside.

Nor is it hard to see why. The vogue for folklore and pseudo-folklore in the United States stands in direct proportion to the vogue of nationalism. And the emphasis on nationalism is in direct proportion to the growth of American influence in world affairs. As Americans have superimposed their cultural and political heritage on other nations, they have felt the necessity of verifying that heritage for themselves. Folklore and pseudo-folklore, often disguised as history, have accounted for group actions, have provided a focal point for group loyalty, have enabled a heterogeneous people to fuse, and have sustained national pride. At the same time, such literature, whether genuine or fake, has served the nostalgia of people living in an industrialized nation where the flow is ever from the rural to the urban and where every year hundreds of "old swimming holes" are filled in to make way for the shopping centers.

In such a situation, it is obvious that popular lore or pseudo-folklore, which can be composed to serve immediate needs and which is more compatible with the culture of America as a whole, is going to be more efficient, more palatable, safer than genuine traditional lore, which originates in ethnic, occupational, or regional interests and which is the product of minds often out of tune with those of the literate American public.

We must, of course, recognize that popular lore, even flying under the false colors of folklore, has served a particularly useful purpose in this nation. A heterogeneous people, emerging from a myriad of ethnic, regional, and linguistic backgrounds, have needed it to attain an element of cultural and political cohesion. Parson Weems' George Washington refuses to lie after cutting down the cherry tree; Abraham Lincoln learns to read by firelight; Davy Crockett hornswoggles his way from the log cabin to Congress and the Alamo. As a nation becoming almost universally literate before its national folk culture could form, America had to provide itself with symbols and legends that other nations would have found ready-made. But we must not forget that this popular lore was, and continues to be, created overnight, to solve immediate needs, and does not spring from tradition but from Madison Avenue, Hollywood, Washington, and the local Chambers of Commerce.

It is American popular lore and American literature, then, not American folklore that the immigrant and the rustic embrace as they cast aside their native culture. It is from popular lore and literature that they discover what being American means, and through popular lore and literature that they will pass this Americanism on to their descendants. The grandmother who speaks only Spanish and lives in an American "Little Mexico," the mother who may speak Spanish but who has gone to school in America and considers English her native tongue, and the daughter who knows no Spanish, is completely American in her ways, and marries a man of German descent make up a representative succession in this nation, as do the suburban college graduate, his city-dwelling parents, and his unlettered Ozark grandparents who are a source of embarrassment to him. Thus, ethnic lores seldom fuse in this country, seldom even have a marked influence upon one another, while regional and occupational lores interact less and less. By the time the folk have left "Little Mexico" or "Little Italy" or the mountains, they have turned toward the literary and sub-literary heritage and may resent any attempts to identify them with the old ways.

In this anthology the arrangement within the various categories of folklore illustrates the stages of its development in America. At the first stage is the immigrant, bringing with him the folklore that is his Old World heritage. At the second stage we see this folklore subjected to the environments of the New World and later to the influence of American popular lore and the literary tradition, with the result that the Old World materials are supplanted or modified. But all the while indigenous regional and occupational lores are emerging. From Jamestown in 1607 to the landing of the most recent immigrant, regardless of his place of birth, this process has continued.

The cycle is not difficult to illustrate. *Saru-to-kani* is a tale widely known in Japan but it was collected near San Francisco, brought there relatively recently by native Japanese. This is folklore at the first stage. "The Flute Player," almost certainly Irish, has been completely localized in Nova Scotia, by a people of Negro and Micmac Indian descent. Hence it is an example of the second stage, as is the crude version of Washington Irving's celebrated short story, "Rip Van Winkle," collected from a Spanish-speaking girl of fourteen in Louisiana. A Dutch song, *Trippa, Troppa, Tronjes* from New York is another instance of folklore in America at the first stage, while "Silver Jack," a recently composed song which had its origin in the lumber camps, is indigenous, but sub-literary in style. A Christmas mummers' play performed in an isolated part of the Kentucky mountains in 1930 and similar to English folk plays dating back to the Middle Ages is another example of the first stage, and a jump-rope rhyme about the Kennedy-Nixon presidential campaign shows the continuing emergence of native American material as well as the adaptation of folk material by persons aware of the nation as a whole.

The content of this book is derived exclusively from the *Journal of American Folklore*, a scholarly periodical published since 1888 by the American Folklore Society. The vast and varied collections it contains include not only American folklore but folklore from every quarter of the globe. It also constitutes a history of the development of the discipline of folklore, revealing through the years a refinement of scholarly technique and reflecting a broadening and an increased firmness of its theoretical assumptions. All too many of the notes on items in this book which were collected a generation or more ago state bleakly that "the place, date, and name of informant are not recorded." Some of the songs provide the words only and not the music. Adequate information about translation is not always forthcoming. However, the new generation of folklorists, rigorously trained and self-conscious about their professional standards, no longer tolerates so cavalier an approach. In fact, some of them are such purists that their collections do not permit comparisons showing what folklore is *not* as well as what folklore is, and do not reveal how folklore evolves from matter which originally was not folklore at all. The inclusion in the present book of sentimental songs such as *La Estrella del Norte* and tales obviously doctored by the collector such as "How the Town Was Named Elkader" make such comparisons possible. For comparative purposes variant versions of riddles and rhymes are also presented. Some of the texts reveal obvious inconsistencies, omissions, and confusion; their inclusion here in so raw a state is designed to demonstrate how folklore, transmitted orally over long periods of time and re-created anew with each telling, actually exists in its natural habitat.

Notes on each entry in this collection are to be found in the back of the book. They include ethnic origin, informant, analogues, types, motifs, bibliographical references, translators, glosses of obscure passages, and other pertinent information.

To the American Folklore Society which graciously permitted us to reprint from the *Journal of American Folklore*, to the folklorists who first gathered this material, and to the often nameless folk who shared their heritage, the editors of this book express their gratitude.

Tristram P. Coffin
Hennig Cohen

University of Pennsylvania
January 1966

THE FOLKTALE

The word *folktale* is not clearly defined in English usage. Rather, it has always been a general term referring to the many types of traditional narrative known to the folk. Men of all kinds have told tales as far back as we can see into history, and they have told tales of all sorts. When they have known how to write, they have written the tales down; when they were unable to write, they passed them on by word of mouth. Tales in written and oral tradition reflect an incessant interchange of material and ideas, and many forms of narrative have come into being. Thus, most folklorists think in terms of the various kinds of folktale and have developed reasonably precise definitions for myth, legend, tall tale, *Märchen,* and so forth.

Primitive myth, when strictly defined, is religious and deals with the creating and ordering of the universe and with an earlier order in which present world conditions were being established. Such myths are still known to the Indians, but had been generally discarded by the Europeans long before they came to this country. More common in the United States are legends dealing with lives and events that are supposed to have taken place in the present order, after present world conditions had been established. Legends are believed by the teller and serve an historical purpose. They differ from the *Märchen* or "fairy tales" which are fictional and take place in a never-never-land and from the tall tales which are meant to be preposterous and spoof the listener. There are also a great number of tales in which rabbits, spiders, foxes, and other ani-

mals play human roles. Some of these tales are mytho-
logical and concern creatures that seem to derive from
a time when, unlike today, the distinctions between
men and animals were not yet present; others simply
use a happy convention that allows animals to talk
and act like humans in the manner of movie cartoons.
And, finally, of course, the folk have a variety of anecdotes, jokes, numskull tales, and personalia which serve
raconteurs the world over.

For most Americans, the Bible serves to explain the
creation and ordering of our universe. Among American folk groups, therefore, myths are not often collected, though pseudo-biblical bric-a-brac such as
"Adam and Eve and Their Children" will turn up from
time to time. Legends like "Shakespeare's Ghost" do
flourish, though generally at the local level, but legends concerning national heroes are usually the sub-
literary creation of superpatriots and sentimentalists.
Animal tales like "Brer Rabbit's Cool Air Swing" and
Märchen like "Valpariso and Lily White" have also
survived in America—in the case of the former, the
stories of the European literary beast cycles mingling
with the Indian and Negro animal trickster tales and
broken-down myths; and in the case of the latter fairy
tales, perhaps first spread by the trappers and priests,
being adopted or preserved by nearly every ethnic
group. However, most American of all, is the tall tale
of which "Big Lies from Grassy" is an example. Tall
tales flourished on the frontier and gave birth to a host
of brawling, drinking, clever champions that typify
what we like to think of ourselves.

For further reading in the folktale, one should go
to the standard text, Stith Thompson's *The Folktale*
(New York, 1946). In this book he will find bibliography, references, descriptions of classification systems—
in fact, all he needs to begin this complicated study.

Turtle Surpasses Man in Ingenuity

It happened thus. Man, whose name was Zomeyo-mebe'e, had a daughter. Now, Man said thus, "No one can ever give me a dowry and marry this virgin of mine for it. She can only be married by the man who brings me water from the stream in a basket." So all men tried to thus win her, but all failed to obtain her in marriage. At last came Turtle one day to Man, saying, "I have come to marry your daughter." Man answered, "Go fetch me basketfuls of water from the stream."

So Turtle made himself a basket. This basket did he take to the stream, where he dipped it into the water. Then he called a child of that village, Man's child it was, and told it thus, "Go tell your father, if he wishes me to carry to him this basketful of water, to make and bring to me a carrying strap of smoke." But Man tired trying to make the carrying strap of smoke, saying at last, "Turtle, you have surpassed me in ingenuity. Come, take and marry my daughter!" So Turtle came and took Man's daughter in marriage. Then lived Turtle and Man many days in great friendship, because Turtle had won Man's daughter by his surpassing ingenuity.

Saru-to-Kani

A crab one day chanced to find a rice cake. An ape, who himself had only succeeded in finding a hard persimmon seed and wanted something which could be eaten immediately, begged the crab to make an exchange with him. The crab agreed and the ape went away munching on his rice cake, thinking what a bargain he had struck. The crab planted the persimmon seed which before long grew into a tall tree with many fruits on its branches. The ape passing by the crab's garden saw the tree, and clambering up the trunk began eating the ripe persimmons. The crab from below asked the ape to throw him some of his own fruit, but the ape only replied by hurling hard green persimmons at the crab who was soon forced to retire into his hole, wounded from the blows.

It happened that the crab was found in this condition by his friends, Rice Mortar, Bee and Chestnut, who upon hearing the crab's story planned a revenge. The crab, as part of the plan, invited the ape to his home, in different corners of which were hidden the plotters, awaiting the ape's arrival. The ape finally appeared, not suspecting any mischief.

Then the fun began! As the ape seated himself by the brazier and lighted the charcoal, out popped the chestnut which, concealed in the brazier, burst open with the heat and struck the ape in the eye, almost blinding him. The ape ran madly into the kitchen seeking to assuage the painful burns when the bee, hidden in the cupboard or pickling barrel, according to some people, darted out and stung him. The ape then dashed for the door, but before he reached it the rice mortar fell upon him from the shelf where it had been lying in wait and pinned the ape down as the crab squeezed his neck with his pincers. The ape realized that he had been wrong and begging pardon, was forgiven by the crab.

Adam and Eve and Their Children

God (*Kihabe*) created the sun and the moon and the stars and the world. He created man and called him Adam. But Adam was not satisfied and God made Eve from one of his ribs. Then he put them in the Garden. He told them not to eat of the fruit of a certain tree. The serpent tempted Eve and they ate. God then told Adam that they

had to work now and that they had to die. And he told
Eve that she had to give birth to her children with pain.

And Eve had twenty-four children. When they grew up
God told Eve to bring out the children to be baptized.
And Eve took only twelve children to be baptized. She
was ashamed and hid twelve of the children in a cave. So
God baptized only twelve of the children.

From the twelve children that were baptized came all
the people that are not Indians, the white people. And
from the twelve that Eve hid in the cave and that were
not baptized came the Indians. When God found out that
Eve had hidden them in a cave he put them in Mount
Blanca (*Piembari*) in Colorado. From there the Indians
came out later and went to the different pueblos. Some
went to Taos, some went to Isleta, some to Sandia, others
to San Juan, and others to Santa Clara and Laguna and
the other pueblos.

The Bear Husband

Once upon a time in a little village in Armenia, there
lived a pretty girl named Mary. One day Mary with some
of her young friends went to the woods to gather food.
The girls were talking and having a fine time when a huge
bear appeared, seized Mary and made off with her. The
girls were so frightened that they threw away everything
they had gathered and ran home as fast as they could and
told Mary's mother what had happened to Mary. The village men organized a party and looked for Mary through
every part of the woods, the mountains, and the near-by
valleys. But she was nowhere to be found. So they came
to the conclusion that she had been eaten by the bear.

The bear took Mary to his den in the mountains and
put a huge stone at the mouth of the cave where he lived
so that no one could come in or go out except himself. He
made Mary his wife, and she bore him a little child who

was a bear. During the first five years Mary lived with the
bear she lost all of her beauty and became black in color,
with heavy hair covering her whole body. Every day the
bear would push away the rock, go out of the den, then
replace the rock and hunt food for the evening meal. He
never forgot to replace the rock, for he was afraid that
Mary would run away from him. One day when he wanted
fresh bread he decided to go to the miller and get some
flour. He left the cave, put the rock at the mouth of it as
usual, then walked to the mill. He went in quietly and
stood before the miller. When the miller looked up and
saw the bear he was terrified, but instead of running away
he waited to see what the bear would do. The bear began
mumbling his request as best he could, but the miller could
not understand. Then the bear gave him a bag and mo-
tioned him to fill it with flour. After the miller had done
so, the bear took the bag, went home to his wife and
ordered her to knead the dough for bread the next morning. She did as he ordered.

When morning came the bear decided to go out and
find some wood with which to bake the bread. In his
haste he forgot after he had passed out, to place the rock
in the entrance of the cave. When Mary saw the opening
and realized that her husband had gone she placed the
baby bear by the rising dough and ran to the village. She
went to her mother's house and knocked on the door.

"Who is it?" her mother asked from within.

"It is your daughter," Mary replied.

"Who is it?" the mother asked again, thinking that she
did not hear aright, because she supposed that the bear
had eaten her daughter.

"It is I, your daughter," Mary replied.

The mother opened the door and saw standing before
her a wild animal. She shuddered! Yet she took her daughter in and scrubbed and scrubbed and scrubbed her. After
having used two cuts of soap, she was still unable to re-
move the grime and dirt which her daughter had collected

in five years. But finally, the mother fed her daughter and put her to bed.

The bear, meanwhile, returned to the cave with the wood and found Mary missing. He began crying, "Manna, manna, kumoruh tootuu-tootuu, chagan laleh-laleh" [Gibberish, supposed to be bear dialect, meaning, "Mary, Mary, the dough is sour, the baby is crying!"], yet his wife did not answer. He repeated his cry several times; but hearing no answer, he decided that he would hurl rocks at the villagers, thinking that they were hiding Mary. So he started rolling large rocks down the mountain into the village and killed several people. Finally, Mary's mother called the village folk together and told them why the bear was rolling rocks down the mountain. "He is angry because Mary ran away from him. But I cannot give her back to him. What are we to do?" she asked.

One of the village youths said, "Don't worry; I'll see what can be done." One day as the bear was again rolling rocks down into the village the youth shot at him. The first bullet did not reach the bear, but the second one did, and the bear tumbled all the way down the mountain, dead.

Several young men skinned the bear and threw the meat into a hole which they dug. As for Mary she never lost her black skin or the hair which covered her body, but continued to look more like a bear than a girl for the rest of her life.

Min Tzŭ Chien

Two thousand years ago there was a son in Shantung Province who was famous for his filial piety. His name was Min Tzŭ Chien, and he was one of the seventy-two disciples of Confucius. His mother died when he was very young. His father married another woman, and two other sons were born to him. The stepmother loved her own sons, and used to give them the best of everything, but the worst to him. This was the evil custom all over China in ancient days.

In China the winter coat was generally made with a layer of cotton batting inside the lining. One winter his father bought enough cotton to make coats for his three sons, and handed it to her. But she put all the cotton in the garments of her own sons, and the dried flowers of rushes in Min Tzŭ Chien's coat.

Neither he nor his father knew this. He always felt cold without understanding why. One day, when there had been a great fall of snow, his father went out for a pleasure-drive with his son, who drove the car. He could not stand such cold weather when he had on but a poor coat of rush flowers. His body shook, and his hand was too cold to hold the reins. After a while the reins fell to the ground, and the horses ran on at a dangerous speed. His father thought that he was lazy, was angered, and took the whip from his hand and beat him with it. His coat was torn by the whip, and the rush flowers were seen by his father. So his father knew that his stepmother had made him a coat out of old cloth and the flowers of rushes. He wept, and said, "That is my mistake; I have made your life miserable by marrying a second wife."

Then Min Tzŭ Chien's father went home, intending to divorce his wife. Min Tzŭ Chien knelt to the ground, and advised his father with a full heart. He said, "As we three brothers would need a mother to bring us up, you would marry another woman if you divorce her. Therefore there would be three sons cold; if you do not, there would be only one son cold. Which way is better?" His father believed his words, and did not divorce his wife. When the stepmother learned the words spoken by Min Tzŭ Chien, she was moved, and after this treated him as kindly as her own sons.

The people of his city learned that he was a wise and good man, and elected him magistrate of the city, but he declined. During that time the Premier of Li (a small county in Shantung Province) was planning to usurp the throne. If Min Tzŭ Chien became the magistrate, he would be compelled to help him. This was why he refused to be the magistrate of his city.

Les Cartes du Nommé Richard

Un jour, c'est un nommé Richard, qui passe devant une église, et entre pour y entendre la sainte messe.

Monsieur Richard s'en va au banc de l'œuvre, comme on y entend et voit le mieux. Là, au lieu de prendre un livre de dévotion de sa poche, il en tire un jeu de cartes. Du doigt le constable lui fait signe de sortir de l'église. Mais monsieur Richard ne remue pas. Le constable vient à lui et dit: "Au lieu de vous amuser avec un jeu de cartes, prenez donc un livre de dévotion." Monsieur Richard lui répond: "Après la messe, je vous donnerai le détail de mon jeu de cartes."

La messe finie, le curé et le constable viennent faire des reproches à monsieur Richard, qui leur répond: "Si vous voulez me permettre, je vais vous expliquer mon jeu de cartes."—"Parle, Richard! répond le curé, je te le permets." Monsieur Richard tire le deux en disant: "Le deux me représente les deux Testaments." Tirant le trois: "Le trois me rappelle les trois personnes de la sainte Trinité: le quatre me représente les quatre évangélistes; le cinq, les cinq livres de Moïse; le six me représente les six jours que Dieu prit à créer le ciel et la terre; et le sept, le jour où il se reposa, après la création." Tirant le huit, il dit: "Le huit me rappelle les huit personnes sauvées du déluge." Tire le neuf. . . . Tire le dix: "Le dix me représente les dix commandements de Dieu." Tire la dame: "Elle me rappelle la reine du ciel." Tire le roi: "Le roi me représente le seul maître à qui je dois obéissance." Tire l'as: "Un seul et même Dieu que j'adore."

Le curé dit: "Monsieur Richard, je m'aperçois que tu as

passé le valet."—"Monsieur le curé, si vous me donnez la
permission de parler, je vous donnerai satisfaction."—
"Parle, Richard! je te le permets."—"Monsieur le curé, le
valet me représente un véritable coquin, comme ici votre
constable devant vous."

TRANSLATION

One day, a man named Richard, who is passing a
church, enters in order to hear holy Mass. Richard goes to
the churchwarden's pew where you hear and see better.
There, instead of taking a book of devotions out of his
pocket, he pulls out a deck of cards. With his finger the
constable makes a sign for him to leave. However, Richard
does not budge. The constable goes up to him and says,
"Instead of amusing yourself with a deck of cards, you
ought to take up a book of devotions."

Richard replies, "After Mass I'll tell you all about my
deck of cards."

The Mass over, the priest and the constable begin to
reproach Richard, who replies to them,

"If you will allow me, I will explain my deck of cards
to you."

"All right, Richard!" replies the priest. "I permit it."

Richard takes the deuce saying, "The deuce is for me
the two Testaments." Taking the trey, "The trey reminds
me of the three persons of the Holy Trinity. The four is
for me the four evangelists; the five, the five books of
Moses; the six is for me the six days that God took to
create the heavens and earth; and the seven, the day on
which he rested after the Creation." Taking the eight, he
says, "The eight reminds me of the eight people saved
from the Flood." He takes the nine . . . [the nine ungrateful lepers]. He takes the ten, "The ten is for me the
Ten Commandments of God." He takes the Queen, "She
reminds me of the Queen of Heaven." He takes the King,

"The King is for me the one Master to Whom I owe obedience." He takes the ace, "The one and same God Whom I adore."

The priest says, "Richard, I notice that you have passed over the Jack."

"Father, if you will give me permission to speak, I will satisfy you."

"Speak, Richard! I permit it."

"Father, the Jack represents a true knave, just like this constable here."

The Priestwife Gets a Beating

Upon a time and once, there was a priestwife and a priest. The priestwife was not of good conduct. She would always say to the priest, "You go to the beets and meets." Once when he went there he met her lover. He was a lyrist. He says to the priest, "Priest, where are you going?" He answers, "The priestwife sent me," he says, "to 'the beets and meets.'" So this lyrist says to the priest, "Your wife is not of good conduct. Her glances are for the street." So they wagered. The lyrist had a red ox, and the priest had forty piasters. So he says, "If the priestwife is such, I'll be giving you forty piasters." The other says, "I'll give you the red ox."

Now he put the priest in a burlap sack. And he takes him and goes to the priestwife. When he went in he says to the priestwife, "Priestwife, don't knock against my sack, my instruments inside might break." When she, the graceful one, saw him, she got up and danced and he made music. And he said in his song:

> "Hear, my sack, hear," he said.
> "My red ox,
> "My forty piasters."

And she sang:

> "The priest I sent
> "To the beets and meets;
> "As he comes back
> "May he break his leg."

So the priest rises out of the sack; he had no more patience and beat her up. The lyrist won the bet.

Now they there and we here better off.

The King and Old George Buchanan

In olden times they was a king (jest a king of the United States, I reckon—that's jest the way they told hit) and they was old George Buchanan, he was called the king's fool, and he didn't like the way the king made the rules. The king made a law that anyone come in and asked him to pardon 'em he'd pardon 'em and not law 'em. George Buchanan didn't like this law, so he kept a-doin' things and then askin' the king to pardon him. Finally at last he come in and told the king to pardon him fer knockin' a man's hat off the bridge and the king did and then George said, "His head was in hit." But the king had done pardoned him and couldn't do nothing. The king told him he'd behead him if he didn't come to the king's house tomorrow at noon, "clothed and onclothed, riding and walking." So George tore one breech leg, one shoe and one sock, one half his shirt. He bridled his old ram sheep and put a saddle on hit and throwed one leg over hit and time of day come he went hoppin' up to the king's door. So the king says, "I thought I told you to come clothed and onclothed and a-ridin' and a-walkin' both." "I did, sir," says George. "Part of me's clothed, part of me's onclothed, one of my legs rode and one walked."

So the king tuk him to be his fool but before he tuk him he went to George's house; wasn't anyone there but

George's sister who was in back room. King says, "Where's your mammy?" and George says, "She tuk some honey to go to town to buy some sweetenin'." (Tuk some honey and went to git some sugar.) He headed the king that way. "Where's your poppy?"—"He's gone to the woods. What he kills he'll throw away and what he don't kill he'll bring back." (He uz picking off lice.)—"What's your sister doin'?"—"She's in the back room mournin' fer what she did last year." (She uz having a baby.) You see George headed the king every time.

So George, he was called the king's fool. So he tried to do one thing and another to make the king make good laws. The king had a law that a man could burn his own house down anytime he had a mind to. So George built a house next to the king's and filled hit with shavin's. King says, "George, what er you doin'?" George says, "I'm fixin' to burn my house." King says, "George, you can't do that, hit'll ketch my house." George says, "Hit's the law." So king says, "If you won't burn hit I'll pay you a good price." George says, "All right, if you make a law that you can't burn a house without you tear hit down and pile hit up." That's the law now.

The king keep a-pardonin' George fer things he'd do, and atter awhile he told him that whatever George wished he could have. So George wished to be the king and the king his fool. So the king says, "George, you headed me all the time, now you got my seat." So George sat up there a while and then give hit back to the king if the king ud promise not to grant nothing until he seed what he was a-grantin'. So the king told him, "Now, George, you leave here and don't you show yourself on Scotland land anymore." So George he left and put England dirt in the bottom of his shoes and got England dirt and put in his hat and he come where they was havin' court, and the king said, "Fetch him here; I told him I'd behead him if he ever stood on Scotland land anymore." And they went and fetched him and he says, "I'm standing on England land

and livin' under England land." So he headed the king agin. And the king never could head George and George never would let the king make no bad laws.

"Jest come to where they was a-holdin' court to law people you know."

Dividing the Chicken

Once there was an old Irish tramp. He came to a farmer's and asked for some dinner. The farmer told him to come in and sit down to dinner. There were a German and a Frenchman there too. The farmer said: "Well, you are the last man to come, you shall cut and serve the chicken." The Irishman agreed, and they brought him a whole chicken. He cut off the head and gave it to the farmer, and said, "You are the head man here, you shall have the head." He cut off the neck and gave it to the farmer's wife, and said, "You are next to the head, so you shall have the neck." He cut off the wings and gave one to each of the two daughters of the farmer, and said, "You will soon fly away from the home nest, and you shall each have a wing." He said to the Frenchman and the German, "You two poor fellows have a long way to go to get home," and gave each of them a foot. Then he said, "I am just a poor old Irish tramp, I'll eat what is left."

An Alsatian Witch Story

The witches held monthly orgies or festivals. In Alsace the chimneys of houses are very wide, and it was through these they left the house without being seen. At a certain farmhouse there were two women—mother and daughter —who were witches. With them lived an inquisitive young farmhand. He had noticed that something unusual was taking place in the house every month, so one night he hid in the kitchen and watched. About midnight the women came and stood naked before the fireplace, beneath the chimney, and after anointing themselves with an oil which the Germans call *Hexenfett* (i.e., witches' fat), uttered some magic words, and up they went through the chimney. The young man then emerged from his hiding place, and seeing the vessel containing the oil, he anointed himself to see what effect it would have on him. He had scarcely pronounced the mystic words when he went up the chimney with a suddenness that was surprising, and when he reached the ground he found himself astride a large black sow which carried him with great speed across the country. They soon arrived at a broad and swift-flowing river, but this did not hinder the onward advance of the sow, for it cleared the broad expanse of water at a single bound. The young man looked back, and, admiring its leaping powers, he said to the sow, "That was a long leap you made," but as he spoke the spell was broken, the sow disappeared, and he found himself in a strange country many miles from home.

Why the Irish Came to America

The King of France he wanted to git married, but he couldn't find no one that suited him. So he went travelin' through the country huntin' a wife. He come to a wilderness where an old hermit monk lived. The king he stayed there awhile with the old monk, and they would go huntin'. One day when they was out a-huntin' they saw three white swans. The king he wanted to kill them, but the old monk said: "No, don't kill them." The king he asked why, and the monk he said, "They ain't swans. They're the girls who come to the lake every day to swim." The old monk had lived a thousand years and he knew all about things.

The king he wanted to catch the three girls. But the

old man said that the only way they could catch them was to git their clothes, and that would be hard to do, for the three women swam so fast that he couldn't git their clothes. But the king kept on insistin' about catchin' the three girls; so the old monk give him a pair of ten-mile boots to put on. The king he put on the ten-mile boots and slipped up to the bank of the lake and stole the three girls' clothes before they knowed it.

Then the girls swam to the shore when they saw what the king had done and they begged for their clothes. But the king wouldn't give them back without they'd take him along with them. The three women they agreed to. The oldest girl took the king first, and she flew away with him and her sisters followed. She carried the king a long way till she came to a mountain, and she dropped him. The second sister she caught him and carried him across the mountain and on a way till she got tired. Then she dropped him. The youngest sister she caught the king and carried him the rest of the way. She was the one the king was goin' to marry.

When they got to the home of the three sisters though, the king he couldn't tell them apart. But the youngest she give him a sign: she held her knees close together, and the other two held their knees apart. And they were married and lived very happy. But the king wanted to go back to France. His wife told him he couldn't, for he would die if he did. He kept on insistin' on goin' back. His wife she finally fixed up a flyin' ship to take him back, but she told him he would die if he got out. The king promised not to git out of the ship, but come straight back.

When the king got to France, he forgot all about what he had promised his wife. He stepped out on the ground and Death was right there, and he nabbed him.

"Don't take me, Death," the king said. "Take these old men around here. I'm young."

"I want you," said Death holdin' on tight to the king.

The king saw that Death was goin' to take him anyhow,

so he said all right he'd go if Death would git in that box he had along. Death got in the box, and the king slammed the lid shut and fastened it tight, so he couldn't git out. The king got in his machine and flew back to his wife.

When the king got back to his wife, he told her what had happened, and he started to open the box Death was in. His wife stopped him and said: "Don't open that box here. If you do we'll all die."

They didn't know what to do with Death. But a storm come up over the ocean, and they took the box with Death in it and dropped it into the ocean. The box floated a long time in the ocean till it come to Ireland and was washed ashore. Men got the box up on the shore and began to wonder what was in it. Two big Irishmen got sledge hammers and broke the box open. Death flew out and killed every man of them. And he started to killin' people all over Ireland. That was why the Irishmen left Ireland and come to America. *The song.*

Remember the song.

Brer Rabbit's Cool Air Swing

Mr. Man he have a fine garden.

Brer Rabbit he visit Mr. Man's garden every day and destroy the lastest thing in it, twell Mr. Man plum wore out with old Brer Rabbit.

Mr. Man he set a trap for old Brer Rabbit down 'longside the big road.

One day when Mr. Man going down to the crossroads, he look in his trap, and sure 'nough, there old Brer Rabbit.

Mr. Man he say, "Oh, so old man, here you is. Now I'll have you for my dinner."

Mr. Man he take a cord from his pocket, and tie Brer Rabbit high on a limb of a sweet gum tree, and he leave Brer Rabbit swinging there twell he come back from the crossroads, when he aim to fotch Brer Rabbit home and cook him for his dinner.

Brer Rabbit he swing thisaway in the wind and thataway in the wind, and he swing thisaway in the wind and
thataway in the wind, and he think he time done come.
Poor old Brer Rabbit don't know where he's at.

Presently here come Brer Wolf loping down the big
road. When Brer Wolf see old Brer Rabbit swinging thisaway and thataway in the wind, Brer Wolf he stop short
and he say, "God a'mighty, man! what you doing up
there?" Brer Rabbit he say, "This just my cool air swing.
I just taking a swing this morning."

But Brer Rabbit he just know Brer Wolf going to make
way with him. Brer Rabbit he just turn it over in his mind
which way he going to get to. The wind it swing poor Brer
Rabbit way out thisaway and way out thataway. While
Brer Rabbit swinging, he work his brain, too.

Brer Wolf he say, "Brer Rabbit, I got you fast; now I
going eat you up." Brer Rabbit he say, "Brer Wolf, open
your mouth and shut your eyes, and I'll jump plum in
your mouth." So Brer Wolf turn his head up and shut his
eyes. Brer Rabbit he feel in his pocket and take out some
pepper, and Brer Rabbit he throw it plum down Brer
Wolf's throat. Brer Wolf he nigh 'bout 'stracted with the
misery. He cough and he roll in the dirt, and he get up
and he strike out for home, coughing to beat all. And Brer
Rabbit he swing thisaway and thataway in the wind.

Presently here come Brer Squirrel. When Brer Squirrel
he see the wind swing Brer Rabbit way out thisaway and
way out thataway, Brer Squirrel he that 'stonished, he
stop short. Brer Squirrel he say, "Fore the Lord, Brer
Rabbit, what you done done to yourself this yer time?"

Brer Rabbit he say, "This yer my cool air swing, Brer
Squirrel. I taking a fine swing this morning." And the wind
it swing Brer Rabbit way out thisaway and way back
thataway.

Brer Rabbit he fold his hands, and look mighty restful
and happy, like he settin' back fanning hisself on his front
porch.

Brer Squirrel he say, "Please sir, Brer Rabbit, let me try your swing one time."

Brer Rabbit he say, "Certainly, Brer Squirrel, you do me proud," and Brer Rabbit he make like he make haste to turn hisself loose.

Presently Brer Rabbit he say, "Come up here, Brer Squirrel, and give me a hand with this knot," and Brer Squirrel he make haste to go up and turn Brer Rabbit loose, and Brer Rabbit he make Brer Squirrel fast to the cord. The wind it swing Brer Squirrel way out thisaway and way out thataway, and Brer Squirrel he think it fine.

Brer Rabbit he say, "I go down to the spring to get a fresh drink. You can swing twell I come back."

Brer Squirrel he say, "Take your time, Brer Rabbit, take your time." Brer Rabbit he take his time, and scratch out for home fast as he can go, and he ain't caring how long Brer Squirrel swing.

Brer Squirrel he swing thisaway and he swing thataway, and he think it fine.

Presently here come Mr. Man. When Mr. Man he see Brer Squirrel, he plum 'stonished. He say, "Oh, so old man, I done hear of many and many your fine tricks, but I never done hear you turn yourself into a squirrel before. Powerful kind of you, Brer Rabbit, to give me fine squirrel dinner."

Mr. Man he take Brer Squirrel home and cook him for dinner.

Valpariso and Lily White

Once upon a time there lived an old miser, way up somewhere near the North Pole, named Mr. Barbab, and he wanted some servants, and a girl named Lily White came along and hired out to him. After some time his wife died and left him alone. His house was filled with all sorts of choice things, bags of gold, and so forth, that he felt he must have a boy to help do the work, as he was getting old.

He hired a boy who came along, named Valpariso. He told him he wanted him to work on the place and do the chores about the house. One morning he sent the boy out to clean the stable and to find a ring (as a test of his faithfulness) that his wife had lost before she died. So he went out with a big barn shovel to clean the stable, but it filled as fast as he shoveled it out, and the harder he worked, the more there seemed to be. The old man had told him not to come back to the house until he found the ring, so when noon came Lily White blew the horn but he dared not go in. After blowing it several times, she went to the stable and found him crying and sobbing, saying the barn filled faster than he could shovel and he could not do the work.

So Lily White, who was a sort of witch, told him that she possessed a secret ring which she could rub and have it do anything for her, so she took the shovel and began to work and soon the stable was cleaned and the ring was found. They went back to the house to eat, and the old man was glad to get the ring and told the boy if he would always work like that and be faithful, he would keep him and pay him well, but if he ever disobeyed him, he would have his life. He was to go to the stable to take care of the horses, Old Blackie, Whitee, and Brownie, and feed the two big black dogs, Bingo and Bango, who were very fierce, to chop the wood, make the fires, lock the house at night, and then he could go to bed.

The next day the old man called him again and told him he had another task for him, and if he was faithful and accomplished the task he would reward him, but if not he would let the dogs bite off his head. He was sent down to the meadows to mow and find a chain which was lost there many years before. The boy went down and began his mowing, but as fast as he mowed, the grass grew up again, and he was discouraged. He worked on, and mowed and mowed and mowed, but he could find no chain.

By and by Lily White slipped out of the house and came down to the meadow to see how he was getting on and found him crying. He said he was afraid to return on account of the master, but he was hungry and felt it was no use to look for the chain any longer. Lily White liked Valpariso and felt sorry for him and told him to sit down and get rested and she would mow a while. So she began her work and at each stroke down went the grass and soon the chain was found. There was great rejoicing then. Valpariso felt that he owed it all to Lily White and began to feel that she was the loveliest creature in the world. She told him that he must be sure and not let the old man know she had helped him, or he would kill her, but to pretend he had found it himself. This he did, and the old man was pleased and called him a smart and faithful boy, but told him to tell him no lies or he would let the dogs eat him up.

Soon after, the old man called Valpariso to him a third time, and told him that he had still another task for him to perform. In the woods near by was a certain tree from which the bark had been stripped and the lower limbs were gone but at the top was a bird's nest with some eggs in it and these eggs he wanted for his breakfast the next day and he must bring them. Valpariso set off to the woods and found the tree easily enough but how was he to climb it? He tried and tried but as the bark was off there was nothing to hold on to, and he kept slipping back. He wished for Lily White. She had helped him before and he felt that she was his only salvation. Lily White was quite busy that morning and found it difficult to slip away, as the old man was very suspicious and kept watching every step she took.

But at last, making some excuse about going for water, she got out of the house and off to the woods and soon came to the tree where Valpariso was. "Well, Valpariso,

how are you getting on?" she called to him. "Oh, Lily
White, I am so glad you have come. Indeed, indeed, I can
never get these eggs and the master will surely kill me
this time." So Lily White thought a while and at last made
a plan. She said, "I will take off my fingers and make pegs
of them for you to climb up on, then you can get the nest,
but you must be very careful and step lightly upon them
or they will break." So Valpariso and Lily White stuck the
fingers in the tree and got the eggs, which he put in his
shirt. But alas! in coming down again he stepped too heavily and the last peg, the little finger of the left hand, was
broken. This grieved Valpariso very much and both were
frightened for fear of the old man.

They went back to the house and Lily White comforted
Valpariso as best she could, saying it did not pain her much
and if only she could conceal it from the old man, all
would go well. The old man was pleased with the eggs
and asked Valpariso how he got them and went through
the same praise and also the same threats if he told him
any lies.

When the time came for dinner, Lily White cooked the
eggs and came in to wait on table, wearing a glove on her
left hand. Soon the old man spied it and asked her what
the matter was. She told him she had burned her hand
but this would not satisfy him and he made her take off
her glove to let him see it. When he saw the broken finger,
he exclaimed, "Ha! I have caught you, you lying witch,
you and Valpariso have cheated me and I will have you
both killed." Poor Lily was frightened and begged that
he would let them go, but the old man was hard and
cruel, and said he would have their lives.

After the dinner dishes were washed, he sent them down
to the cellar to get two big soap kettles which were there
and to fill them with lye and put them over the stove. He
set the dogs to watch them so they could not run away.
Then he called for his wine which Lily White mixed for
him and made it very strong. After he had drunk it, he

told them to go down into the cellar and jump into the kettles, Valpariso in one and she in the other, and that they would be boiled into soap.

Valpariso was very much frightened, for they could not escape on account of the dogs which the old man had unchained. Lily White told him they must pretend to do just as the old man said, but she thought they might outwit him as she had given him so much wine. She knew where he kept the keys and she got them. She had prepared the kettles of lye over the fire as he had told her, but they would not jump in. She got some meat for the dogs and poisoned it. They ate it greedily and were soon quiet. Then she, with Valpariso to help, lifted one dog into a kettle, telling Valpariso to cry and scream as she did so to make the old man think it was he, and then they would put the other dog in and she would cry and scream herself.

By this time the old man was too drunk to move and only laughed and swore while he supposed they were being scalded. After all was quiet, he fell into a drunken slumber. Then Lily White stole silently upstairs, and, watching her chance, stole his keys and opened the chest where the gold and money were kept and took as much as both could carry. Then they went to the stable and stole the white horse which was the fleetest and best in the stable, and, both mounting upon it, they rode away.

The Flute Player

My grandfather was named Peter Pennall. In those old-fashioned days he was a man that believed in a good angel and a bad angel. The bad angel had him led that he could do more than a common man in many points. He was a fifer. He went up on Le Havre River moose huntin'. One calm evenin' he made up his mind to make a kind o' blind to keep the dew off himself, an' stay all night. He made it out o' brush. Then he made a fire an' put a kittle o' water over the fire, an' started restin'. He made some tea. (In those days they picked the hemlock an' the yellow birch brush an' steeped that, an' make tea out of it. That's a kind o' tonic for the stomach, an' yet it was somethin' to drink.) So nicely the[y] started playin' some old tunes. The first one was an Irish tune "Schissle le Bri." Next he played "Cock in the North." Then he played "Lord MacDonald's Reel." After that he played "Denny O'Shann." Then he stopped an' laid his flute down. By that time the water was warm enough for him to fix up his drink. So he made up his mind to have tea. While he was stirring around here, he was way in the woods quite a while. First thing he hears a fife playin' a strange tune. The last tune that was played was "MacDonald's Reel." My grandfather said, "Bless me, I'm way out here all alone. I wouldn't mind havin' some company here tonight. That fellow will have to come here an' we'll play together." Pretty soon he heard footsteps an' woods crackin', an' the leaves. A man knocked on the door an' come in. He had a little parcel under his arm. He said to my grandfather, "Good evening." My grandfather replied, "Good evening, sir, come right in. You must stay with me for the night." The man said, "Oh, no, but what is your name?"—"Peter Pennall," said my grandfather. "Well, Peter," said the stranger, "I heard you this evenin' playin' your flute. Then I started playin' mine. You're an awful good player, Peter. What do you think o' mine?" My grandfather said, "You do very well, sir, but you must stay with me tonight and we will play together." The stranger said, "No, I can not stay with you tonight; but here's a suit o' clothes, seein' you're a poor man an' might be needin' o' these. If you put these suit o' clothes on, they'll be nothin' you can't do. Not sayin' I'm comin' for fair, or nothin', but if you don't put those suit on, you won't have no luck an' you'll be a cripple." My grandfather became very angry. He said to the man, "You can take those clothes on with you, I'll not wear them. You can stay here tonight if you want, or if you've a mind to

git out you kin take your feet right out o' here." The man
left, an' a short time after that my grandfather became a
cripple. He was a cripple for the rest of his days.

The Mean Rich Man

Once there were a rich man, very mean, and he think
all the time how to fool the mens who work for him, and
get them to work too hard for little money. So one day he
goes to the town, and he sees a simple man standing in
the street, not doing nothing, so (with his mouth open).
He go up to him and say, "You want to work?" and the
simple man says, "Sure," and he say, "Come up to my
place, and I give you fifty cents a day." And the simple
man he says, "Sure," and the rich man laugh to hisself,
and think, "O now I get this simple man to work hard."

So they get to this rich man's house, and it too late to
work, so in the morning he wake him up and say, "Hey,
you got to go to the fields to work." So the simple mans
get up and he eat a good breakfast, the rich man's wife
give it to him. And the rich man say, "You got to go far to
work, over fields, too far to come home for lunch." So
the simple man say, "You give me my lunch now. I want
it now so no one have to come after me with my lunch."
And the rich mans too glad, he give him the lunch so that
no one has to stop work to go give the simple man eat.
And when the simple man finished, the rich man say, "O
why don't you eat your supper now so you don't have to
come home early?" He think he can't eat much now, and
then his wife don't have to give him to eat after.

So the simple mans said, "All right," and he eat his supper. Then the rich man say, "Now go to the field to work,"
and the simple man say, "O no, all my life after supper
I go right to sleep. All my life I have a habit, not change
now." And he go to sleep, and the rich mans too mad.

Wait Till Emmett Comes

Once upon a time there was an old colored preacher who was riding to a church he served at some distance from his home when night overtook him and he got lost. As it grew darker and darker, he began to be afraid, but he bolstered up his courage by saying every little while, "De Lawd will sholy take care ob me." By and by he saw a light, and riding up to it, he discovered that it came from the cabin of another colored man. Getting off his horse and tying it to a fence stake, he knocked at the cabin door. When the owner opened it, the old preacher told his trouble and asked to stay all night. The colored man replied, "Well, Pahson, I suttinly would like ter keep yo' all night, but my cabin hain't got but one room in it an' I got a wife an' ten chilluns. Dey jis' ain't no place fo' yo' ter stay."

The old preacher leaned up against the side of the house and in a woebegone voice said, "Well, I guess de Lawd will sholy take care ob me." Then slowly untying his horse and getting on him, he started to ride on. But the owner of the cabin stopped him and said, "Pahson, yo' might sleep in de big house. Da' ain't nobody up da' an' de doo' ain't locked. Yo' can put yo' hoss in de ba'n an' give him some hay an' den you can walk right in. You'll fin' a big fiahplace in de big room an' de wood all laid fo' de fiah. Yo' can jis' tech a match to it an' make yo'self cumfable." As the old preacher began to disappear into the dark, the other called out, "But, Pahson, I didn' tell you dat de house is hanted." The old man hesitated for a moment, but finally rode away, saying, "Well, I guess de Lawd sholy will take care ob me."

When he arrived at the place, he put his horse in the barn and gave him some hay. Then he moved over to the house, and sure enough, he found it unlocked. In the

big room he found a great fireplace with an immense
amount of wood all laid ready to kindle. He touched a
match to it and in a few minutes had a big roaring fire.
He lighted an oil lamp that was on a table and drawing
up a big easy chair, he sat down and began to read his
Bible. By and by the fire burnt down, leaving a great heap
of red-hot coals.

The old man continued to read his Bible until he was
aroused by a sudden noise in one corner of the room.
Looking up, he saw a big cat, and it was a black cat, too.
Slowly stretching himself, the cat walked over to the fire
and flung himself into the bed of red-hot coals. Tossing
them up with his feet, he rolled over in them, then shaking
the ashes off himself, he walked over to the old man and
sat down to one side of him, near his feet, looked up at
him with his fiery-green eyes, licked out his long, red
tongue, lashed his tail, and said, "Wait till Emmett
comes."

The old man kept on reading his Bible, when all at
once he heard a noise in another corner of the room, and
looking up, he saw another black cat, big as a dog. Slowly
stretching himself, he walked over to the bed of coals,
threw himself into them, tumbled all around, and tossed
them with his feet. Then he got up, shook the ashes off
himself, walked over to the old man, and sat down near
his feet on the opposite side from the first cat. He looked
up at him with his fiery-green eyes, licked out his long,
red tongue, lashed his tail, and asked the first cat, "Now
what shall we do wid him?" The first cat answered,
"Wait till Emmett comes."

The old man kept on reading his Bible and in a little
while he heard a noise in a third corner of the room, and
looking up, he saw a cat black as night and as big as a
calf. He, too, got up, stretched himself, walked over to the
bed of coals, and threw himself into them. He rolled over
and over in them, tossed them with his feet, took some
into his mouth, chewed them up and spat them out again.

Then shaking the ashes off himself, he walked over to the old colored man and sat down right in front of him. He looked up at him with his fiery-green eyes, licked out his long, red tongue, lashed his tail, and said to the other cats, "Now what shall we do wid him?" They both answered, "Wait till Emmett comes."

The old preacher looked furtively around, slowly folded up his Bible, put it into his pocket, and said, "Well, gemman, I suttinly is glad to hab met up wid yo' dis ebenin', an' I sholy do admire fo' to had yo' company, but when Emmett comes, you tell him I done *been* heah an' hab done *went*."

The Man Who Plucked the Corberie

In a large logging camp in the Maine woods, a crew of loggers were chopping for a logging company and under the leadership of a very cruel and brutal man named John who was known to be able to beat up five to six men any time at the least provocating word or act. One night or early morning during a severe snowstorm the men were in camp drinking or playing cards not having been able to even step outside the doors for three days. These men used to very active work were all in a very bad temper, but none so bad as Big John, the camp boss; and Pierre LeBlanc, the camp cook, who was the smallest man in camp and who was always stating that some day he, Pierre, would beat the life out of Big John, to which all would joke about; on this particular stormy night Big John was sitting by a window, when a little corberie came to peck on the window pane wanting to be let in out of the cold. Big John opened the window, and taking the corberie in, proceeded to clean off every last feather; then tossing the bird back in the cold night. The men stared in frightful awe at this cruel act, none daring to speak a word except little Pierre. Pierre, tiny alongside Big John, stepped in

front of the cruel man and denounced him as only a
Frenchman can do and then made his last threat to Big
John. "John, you big brute, some day you will wake up
and you will also be plucked clean of every last hair on
your body."

In the early morning the men were awakened by an
awful moan. Then tramping on the floor getting out of
bed they saw an awful sight; Big John, the cruel and the
brute of all the logging camps, was pacing the floor stark
naked, and as hairless as the little bird had been feather-
less. At this time little Pierre came from his kitchen and
taking one look at Big John said, "Now you big strong
brutal animal, God has punished you, but not the way
Pierre is going to do." And with that he proceeded to give
the big man the most unholy beating anyone had ever
witnessed and every man stood rooted to the floor unable
to stop Pierre until Big John was whimpering and crying
like a baby. When Big John was revived Pierre fixed him
a lunch and ordered him out of the camp with the warning never to return.

From that day on no man in the Maine and New Brunswick camps would work for the once big woods boss, so
the company passed a rule that Big John would have the
rights to food and lodging for one night at any of their
camps; and Big John earned his keep going from camp to
camp, not daring to stay more than one night and making
reports to the logging company on location of good wood
lots that could be had for logging.

Big Lies from Grassy

"Airy news from Grassy?"

"Nope. We hain't had nothing behappen since John
Will Jarles got drunk tuther night."

"Sure nuf? What did he do?"

"We wuz sittin' by the fire tuther night when he tried

to ride his mule in the door. He kept yellin', 'It's the end
of the world. I seed Satan on the mountain.' We got him
offen the mule, then he fell inter the beehive. He sobered
up then, I tell ye."

"Is he in town? John Tom 'lowed he wanted ter see
him."

"He's down ter the store, I reckon, a-tellin' some big
lie. He got the prize tuther night fer tellin' the biggest."

"What was it about, the billy goat?"

"Nope. He claimed ter have climbed a tall tree ter
heaven. Accordin' to him, day coming on, John Tom
awoke and laced up his boots afore going ter mill. Whilest
his old woman made the biscuit, he caught up his old
mule Bare Bones and saddled her. Knowing his ways, the
old woman 'lowed he orter go by Crackers Neck ter
miss the mudhole. John Tom 'lowed that he'd be back afore
night came on and not git stuck either; but jest as he got
outsides the gate Bare Bones' back broke into with a snap.
Well, sir, he study what he goin' ter do, then he took his
knife and a chestnut limb and whitled the purtiest backbone yer ever did see, so it fited in the mule's back. John
Tom was ready ter go on; but a tree sprouted up way, way
beyond the blue (out of the chestnut he had for the mule's
backbone). It grew and it grew. I tell you it was some
tree. As he couldn't see the top, John Tom climbed up ter
see whar it went. He looked down and he couldn't see the
ground, then he looked up and seen what looked ter be
a rail fence, only the rails were of ivory and jasper. At
the little white gate stood an old man in a white robe.
John Tom 'lowed it must be heaven. Whilst he was study-
ing what ter do St. Peter called, 'Come on in and git ter
work.' Hit was a sight ter see the big level fields with
bands of angels, some planting corn with golden hoes and
some picking the harp. Well, sir, John Tom took a hoe and
went ter work with the rest of them as big as life. Over
in a corner Gabriel, Moses, and Timothy played ring-
around-the-roses. One of the angels brung a gold jug with

the purtiest water from the branch you ever seed. He took it and lay down in the shade of the fence where he could see the tree that growd from Bare Bones' back. John Tom got ter thinking about his old woman and the cabin on Wells Creek. Looking down, down towards the earth, he saw his old woman a-lookin' up. She war mad sure nuf 'case she wanted him ter fetch the meal fer ter make bread.

"'You come down,' she yelled.

"'I cain't, you come up,' he answers.

"'John Tom, yer come home and care fer yer wife and young uns 'er I'll skin ye.'

"With that he gave one last look at heaven, and begun ter climb down. Being light-headed he stepped out too fer on a branch and down fell John Tom head first. He lit on a big stone nigh the mill. His head was in so tight the miller couldn't pull him loose no way he tried. So his woman come up with an ax and cut it off.

"Then John Tom set there looking sorta dazed. 'Where's Gabriel?' he asked. 'What yer want with him?' asked the miller sorta laughing behind his hand. The old woman 'low he hain't got good sense since his fall. Well, sir, they got the meal ground someway and the last the miller seen of him he was carrying the poke hoe home peck-a-back."

"Surenuf, that's a good un. It minds me of some grandsir uster tell."

"What were they about? I won't name it to a soul."

"First one thing then tuther. We uster favor the one about the fox."

"Name it, won't yer?"

"I cain't, I disremember."

"I know where there's a quart of licker hid."

"Well, it was way back in the eighties, so grandsir said. One January day come a blizzard, the wind was blowing big guns. It was a good time ter hunt down a fox beast that had been bothering the chickens. So he and grandsir went out with Long Tom, Short Tom, and Sweet Mary Jane. 'At top of Tater Knob,' says grandsir, 'I gave my horn a blow fer I seed a beast hidin' behind a big stone. The dogs come a-runnin' just as it frisk atop, its brush as big as a poke and blue, the purtiest blue yer ever seed. I hated ter but Uncle Joe let fly at it, and, young uns, hit musta been bewitched. The shot went through it like air. Then hit leaped over the dogs easy like, and was off thirty feet at a jump. Uncle Joe built us a fire, and we passed the time with a quart of licker.

"'Pretty soon Sweet Mary Jane and tuther dogs slunk back like we knowed they would, nary a dog on earth could catch such a fox critter. We started home through the snow, when what should we meet but the critter friskin' around a big tree trunk, eyes as big as dishpans. I set down and pulled a spike outa my shoe heel. Then I slipped around and nailed the brush of the critter to the tree trunk. Uncle Joe lit a pine knot and waved it in front of its eyes. The fox beast scrambled out of its skin and was gone. Hit musta been cold without the kiverin'. Hit was a sight ter see maw when we brought in the skin. Hit filled the whole room. We cut it up into twenty-nine small skins and sold them to a travelin' hawker fer nigh three dollars each. Takin' hit all in all hit payed us ter go huntin' in the cold. I hain't been nigh Tater Knob since.'"

A Numskull Story

A nitwit was standing by the depot watching a train go by. One flat car was loaded with large sewer tiles. As they passed, the boy nudged a bystander and said, "What's *them?*" Thinking that he would have a little fun, the man questioned replied, "Them's *traveling postholes!*"

The stupid boy grinned and continued to watch the passing freight. About seven or eight cars behind the sewer tiles came one loaded with long heavy railroad ties. At this, the boy pulled the man's sleeve and said, "Yep, them *were* the postholes. There go the posts!"

The Preacher and the Hog

Once a certain preacher, when he ran shy of meat, went out in the thicket near his house and killed one of his neighbor's hogs (hogs at that time ran at large). And he and his wife dragged it to their yard to clean it. But just as they were getting through with the gutting, they looked up and saw two old women coming over the hill, their staves in their hands, on their way to meeting. And they were coming right to the preacher's own house, for he had appointed meeting at his house for that day. On seeing the old women (who were getting to meeting ahead of time), the preacher and his wife carried the hog into the house and, for lack of a better place to put it, pushed it under the bed.

The people gathered, and the meeting went along fine till all of a sudden the preacher in the middle of his sermon spied one of the hog's legs a-sticking out from under the bed curtains. He then bided his time till they "heisted" a hymn. And, when he could catch his wife's eye, he would put into the hymn, where the congregation wouldn't notice, some lines for only his wife to hear. They went like this:

> "Oh, Glory, Allelulia!
> Oh, push that sow's leg under the bed.
> Oh, Mattie, don't you hear me?"

While the song was still going on, a couple of hound sluts came in and started nosing around the bed; so the preacher put in something like this:

> "Git out o' here, you flop-eared houn',
> Glory, Allelulia.
> For if you don't, I'll knock you down,
> Glory, Allelulia."

Rip Van Winkle

Once there was a man who lived with an old woman.
The man would never want to work and his wife would
always beat him. One day he got tired of being beaten
and nagged.

So he took his shining gun and his dog and went out to
the mountainside. He saw many funny people out there.
He fell asleep and when he awoke, he reached for his
shining gun, but a rusted one was there instead. He called
his dog, but no dog appeared. He did not see it.

He looked for his friends; they were all gone. He began
to get up and his bones were all cracking. He began to
slap his face which was an old habit of his; and instead
of finding a smooth face, he found a long beard. He
seemed like a stranger. He asked about his best friend,
and they told him he was dead these eighteen years. A
boy and girl making way to him was daughter and son.
They told him his wife had been dead a long time. They
all went back to their home and lived happily ever after.

Rip Van Winkle sat down each evening and told stories,
but the one he told most was the one about himself.

Juan José

Encontrábase un día un portorriqueño en los Estados
Unidos. El no sabía inglés ni los americanos el español.
Iba por el camino y vió una preciosa casa; acercóse y díjole
al portero:—¿De quién es esa casa? El criado le dijo:—
What do you say? El portorriqueño se creyó que el portero
le había dicho que "Juan José."

Siguió caminando; vió un palacio y le preguntó al
hombre que estaba allí:—¿De quién es ese palacio?—

What do you say?—*le respondió el hombre.—¡Vaya por Dios, de Juan José!—dijo el portorriqueño.*

Vió un ventorrillo y preguntó de quién era aquel ventorrillo con tan ricos frutos. El hombre le contestó:— What do you say? Y *el portorriqueño se figuró de nuevo que era de Juan José.*

*Siguió caminando y vió un grupo de gente y se figuró que estaba peleando y preguntó:—¡Oh! ¿qué es eso? ¿Quién está peleando? Y un americano le dijo:—*What do you say?—¡Ah! peleando Juan José.

Vió un carro fúnebre y preguntó:—¿Quién se murió?— What do you say?—¡Ah! Juan José se murió.

Vió a un amigo y le dijo:—Oye, se ha muerto un señor llamado Juan José, que posee todo lo de los Estados Unidos y quería poseer todo pero no pudo.

Translation

One day a Puerto Rican found himself in the United States. He didn't understand English and the Americans didn't understand Spanish. He went along the street and saw an expensive house. He went up to it and said to the porter,

"Whose house is this?"

The servant said to him, "What do you say?"

The Puerto Rican believed that the porter had said "Juan José" to him.

He walked on. He saw a palace and asked the man who was there, "Whose palace is this?"

"What do you say?" replied the man.

"My God, not Juan José!" said the Puerto Rican.

He saw a tavern and asked who owned such a profitable tavern. The man answered him, "What do you say?" And again the Puerto Rican thought it was Juan José.

He walked on and saw a small group of people and believing they were fighting asked, "What is all this? Who is fighting?"

And an American said to him, "What do you say?"

"Ah, Juan José fighting!"

He saw a funeral procession and asked, "Who has died?"

"What do you say?"

"Ah, Juan José has died."

He saw a friend and said to him, "Alas, a man called Juan José has died—this fellow who owned all of the United States and who wanted to possess everything but was unable to."

The Fire-Hunt

"This is a monstrous nice night to shine old bucks' eyes, Uncle Billy; s'pose we take a fire-hunt," said a quiz to the old man, to draw out of him the reasons that caused him to leave the Huckleberry Ponds of Cumberland.

"It mout be," said Uncle Billy, with his white, leaden eyes looking very sorrowfully, "but I don' 'clude I'll fire-hunt no more. That drefful night that caused me to leave good ole Cumberland I shall never forgit. That wur the wust fire-hunt a poor mortal ever got inter. It was a dark, drizzly night—good night fur jacker-mer-lanterns and old bucks. I took O'Pan, loaded her heavy with big drop shot, which I bought in Fayetteville with huckleberries, with pan and torch on a shoulder; got lost—led out'n my way by a stinkin' jacker-mer-lantern. I went bogin along, thought I was gwine right, looked afore me, seed a whole heap o' bright shiny eyes, turned the pan round and round. 'Shiny eyes—shiny eyes,' says I; 'now's the time! now's the time!'

"I whip up O'Pan, draw a bead—bang! went O'Pan; jingle, jingle, jingle went chains. I see men comin'; I throw down O'Pan, light, and all, and took through the huckleberry swamp like a 'coon. Here come men arter me, sayin', 'Here he goes, boys! here he goes!'

"I run on, come to mudpond, and in I went, sock! sock! sock! last up I go to my armpits, and could go no furder. Men come up and say, 'Here he went, boys! here he went!'

"I lay in the mud, still as a turkle, till they lost me. When they left me I tried to git out—had a hard time of it. Thar stood a jacker-mer-lantern grinnin' at me. I rake mud, fust with one hand, then with t'other—rake, rake. Last out I cum, muddy as a hog. I went home, told the fambly, left that night, fambly follered, and all the poor men got for my shootin' thar hosses was O'Pan and my torch pan. That was a mem'ble night—never forgit—never fire-hunt since."

Shakespeare's Ghost

Woman went to Shakespeare's grave. He did come back, and talk to her. Song was a conversation they had. When he first come back he said:

1. "Bring me a note from the dungeons deep,
   And water from a stone;
   And lily-white milk from a female's breast,
   For a fair maid never had none."

She said:

2. "One kiss, one kiss from your clay-cold lips,
   One kiss is all I crave;
   Just one kiss from your pale, cold lips,
   Then return back to your grave."

He said:

3. "If I was to give to you one kiss,
   Your days would not last long;
   For my lips are eaten with the worms,
   And my breath is earthly strong."

Used to be an English settlement in Chatsworth. They

came there about 1861, when the railroad first come in.
[Some of their names were] Acres, Brooks, Eliots,
Humphries. Fellow name of Elwagon sung that. He come
direct from England. He said that Shakespeare was a
great lover. He married this woman. After he was married two or three years, there was another man fell in love
with his wife, but she didn't care nothin' about him. This
man hired four or five men to kidnap Shakespeare. They
took him up into a room and castrated him. Well, his
wife said it didn't make any difference to her, she wanted
to live with him. He said no, it couldn't be; he couldn't
live with her no longer because he wasn't a man. He
coaxed her to go into a convent, and after a while she
consented and went in. Two or three years afterwards he
died—Shakespeare died pretty young. After he died, she
got out of this convent. She used to go to his grave and
pray for him to raise—she wanted to speak to him—see
him. And this song was made up about that. This song
is founded on fact.

Stories about Mr. Mac

The central figure was always the husband and father,
Mr. Mac (he was not a Mac, actually, but his surname
was as Scottish as if he had been), a prosperous farmer;
the other members were merely subsidiaries or, perhaps
rather, victims.

The most conventional of the tales concerns the father's
order that his sons, on the infrequent occasions when
they were wearing new shoes, should take especially long
steps. The mother, it was sometimes added, finally obtained a withdrawal of this injunction by pointing out
that it involved a serious danger of splitting their trousers.

A very similar story immediately comes to mind, included in Margaret Wilson's novel of a Scottish family
in Iowa in the 1860s, *The Able McLaughlins* (New York,

1923). Andy McFee, even in his prosperous old age, persisted in removing his shoes when they were not currently needed for walking purposes "till an able granddaughter-in-law urged him not to misuse shoestrings with such extravagance."

Another similar story, which, however, lacks the element of feminine intervention, has the father say, prior to departing on a journey: "An', wife, see that wee Wullie tak's off his glasses when he's no lookin' at onything!"

My mother, to whom I recently applied for a check on my recollections, supplied a story which was new to me, probably because [it was] lacking in the dramatic qualities of those which I did remember. It was merely that Mr. Mac, discovering that to start his car in the conventional fashion required an undue amount of "gas," used to require his wife and hired man to start it by pushing.

One of the most popular of the stories was of how the man of the house, going the rounds of the stores in search of cracked eggs, stale bread, and wilted vegetables, finally approached the butcher shop. He glanced up at the swinging sign above the door—which represented a side of bacon—checked a moment for a second glance, and entered, his brow furrowed with thought. He poked, priced, and depreciated the meats on display, but it was evident that his true interest lay elsewhere. "That side of bacon over the door," he finally remarked, "—how often do you change it?" The butcher, a gamesome character, immediately saw where the wind lay. "Why, about every year, I guess—and now that you mention it, I believe the year is just about up." "Well, in that case, how about taking it down and letting me have it?—it wouldn't be worth anything to you after hanging up there all that time in the rain and sun and dust and flies." "Oh I could hardly do that!" demurred the butcher. "It ought to be worth something to somebody. . . ." After protracted bargaining, a sufficiently depreciated price was finally agreed upon, the "side of bacon" taken down, wrapped and de-

livered, and payment made. The thrifty farmer returned
it next day, more in sorrow than in anger. It was, of course,
an ingeniously painted slab of wood.

I heard this story so early in my childhood that it was
with a "shock of recognition" amounting almost to out-
rage that I encountered a similar situation in one of the
juvenile publications I favored—probably the *American
Boy*. In this case, however, the transaction involved a ham
—of sawdust-stuffed canvas—which a smart-aleck clerk sold
to an aged farmer—not as a bargain but rather as a particularly fine piece of merchandise, hung thus to acquire
flavor. The moral, I believe, was that clerks should not
play practical jokes on customers. It is unlikely that the
American Boy story · could have been based upon this
piece of local folklore and the contrary could not, in this
case, have been true. Were both derived from a common
origin or was the published story merely a case of art
unconsciously imitating nature? I know only that I felt
that the published story was itself "damaged goods."

My favorite deals with the father settling his monthly
bill at the general store. "Right!" the storekeeper exclaimed. "Thank you very much! And now, if you'll wait
just a minute, I'll put up a sack of candy for the children"
—as was the genial custom in those days at a settlement
of accounts. Mr. Mac put up a restraining hand. "If it's
all the same to you," he said, "I think I'll just have the
worth of it in assorted nails!"

Mr. Mac here appears as a distant relative of the man
who, on Christmas Eve, went out into the backyard, fired
off a pistol, and rushed into the house to inform his children that Santa Claus had just committed suicide.

The final tale deals with a period when Mr. Mac, long
since retired from the farm and mellowed by years and
prosperity, yielded to his wife's urgings and built a fine
large house. The ruling passion, however, temporarily
stifled, then returned in full force. The house completed
and ready for occupancy, Mr. Mac drew the line at buying

appropriate new furniture; instead he personally moved the old furniture into the new house—under cover of night, with his wife's assistance, by handcart! That he did not do so in full daylight—as he had formerly bargained for wooden sides of bacon and requested the substitution of nails for candy—may, however, be taken as suggesting a weakening of his moral fiber.

How the Town Was Named Elkader

A queer tale goes about: Abt El Kader, after deeds of heroism in remote Africa, lent his name to this Iowa village that it might be a place of courage. A story like all the answers grownups give when they don't understand the question. For of course, what really happened is this:

Long and long ago, before there were houses, in the Turkey valley umber tepees blended here and there against the rocky background. Things weren't much different otherwise, a little quieter, perhaps. Indians liked this place. For treasures they had colored leaves, and their little princess, the finest princess in the world. She loved the hills. "You must never go up in them alone," the chief said. And she did not mean to disobey. But one day, cedars laughed in the sunlight, oaks beckoned, and the birches bent far down and waved. Laughing, too, she went to meet them. High in the hills, *an elk ate her*. That is how the town was named.

Elks not carnivorous? Have you looked at hills a November evening: every leaf ripped from the trees, color drained from grass and sky, and no snow fallen yet to heal the scars, . . . so there are only rocks cutting through naked hill-flesh? Have you watched hills suffering in November twilight? No? Then maybe you cannot understand how cruel they have had to grow to find strength for their own pain, and how all their mild summer beauties are twisted laughs flung back at Fate. Underneath they are tortured and writhing, exacting hardness from their visitors, vengeance of their dwellers. Does it seem strange that an elk in such hills learned to eat human flesh?

Night Doctors

I.

There was an employment office for colored girls down at Twelfth and Lombard Streets which became the talk of the town a few years ago. It was run by Mrs. Logan. I knew her, often saw her walking along the streets, and in trolley cars. . . . The girls were supposed to be going to jobs, but everybody knows now that these girls just disappeared. If you tried to trace the girls you would find their trunks at some place where the girls were supposed to be sent, but no girls. . . . They were sent to hospitals and the doctors cut them up.

II.

I remember a colored lady was going to work early in the morning, about half past five o'clock. She was standing at Twelfth and Market Streets when an automobile came up. A man in the automobile spoke to her, "Mary, which way are you going? I'll take you where you want to go in a hurry. The trolleys are all blocked." But the lady wouldn't get in the automobile. The man kept on insisting, and the woman became frightened. Just then a colored man across the way saw her and started towards her. At that the man in the automobile left. He was a night doctor and was going to take the lady to a hospital.

The Soldier Who Used His Head

During a mopping-up operation an army rifleman spotted a Jap sniper hiding in a rocky cleft in the side of a knoll. He drew a bead on him but the Jap jumped up and took off just as he fired. He missed the Jap by inches and this made him so mad he took right out after him though there were probably other snipers in the area. This knoll was a rugged volcanic outcropping and there were plenty of clefts and cracks and the Jap kept dropping into one, bobbing up and then wriggling over into the next one. He was fast as a squirrel and the American couldn't get a shot at him. Besides the Jap kept taking a potshot of his own now and then and the Yank had to hug the rocks pretty close himself.

But he kept after the Jap and pretty soon they'd worked clear around the knoll to where they were before. The GI wasn't going to let the little bastard get away so he did his best to work closer. But the Jap kept ahead of him and they went on around the knoll again. They went clear around that knoll seven times.

By that time the soldier was getting pretty disgusted and so he did something the Japs were never taught to do—he used his head. He whanged the barrel of his rifle against a rock and bent it into a half circle. Then he drew a fine bead on where the Jap's body would be when he wriggled out of the hole he was in then. The Jap was naturally out of sight at that moment but the Yank knew what he was doing and he fired anyway. The bullet went around and around the knoll sixteen times because of the barrel being bent in a circle, you see. Then the Jap rolled up and out and over toward the next hole. When he got in the path of the bullet it hit him and killed him. The soldier put in for a medal but he didn't get it because there were no eye-witnesses to what he'd done. Of course everybody in his outfit believed him anyway.

The Three Chaplains Play Cards

Three chaplains in the army were sitting in a tent, playing cards to pass the time away, and idly discussing the subject of honesty. The Protestant and the Catholic insisted that lying was sometimes necessary; the Jew maintained that in all cases, lying was sinful. Suddenly, the commanding officer walks into the tent. The three chaplains hurriedly hide the cards. The CO asks the Catholic chaplain, "Father Murphy, were you playing cards? You know my orders against card playing." The Catholic answers no. The CO turns to the Protestant and the minister says no, he wasn't playing cards. Then the officer turns to the Jew. "Chaplain Goldfarb, were you playing cards?" "Mit who?"

Using the Telephone

Another story is told about the first telephone line which was installed in National Mine, about three or four miles from Ishpeming [Michigan]. This happened years ago and when the line was extended a phone was installed in the store, in the doctor's office, in the mine office, and in the captain's home. The captain, as you know of course, is the man in charge of actual operations at a mine. Next door to the captain lived a miner by the name of Johnnie Rowe. He had a large family. They were grown up and all away from home and one of the daughters lived in Ishpeming.

Mrs. Rowe went into Ishpeming one day to visit her daughter. It was a nice day and she hung the carpets and the drapes out to air while she was away. Some time after she arrived in Ishpeming it started to rain and thunder and lightning and she said to her daughter, "Mary Jane, I shall 'ave to go 'ome." And the daughter asked, "Ow, mother?" "Well," said mother, "I got they carpets and they curtains 'anging on the line. Your father wan't knaw enough to put them in." "Well, mother," the daughter said, "You don't 'ave to go 'ome. We got one they new telyphones. You can call up Captain Broad, 'e have a tely-phone and 'e can go over and tell faather and faather can come to the phone and you can tell 'im what to do." So they called up Captain Broad and he went over to Mr. Rowe and said, "Johnnie, comez on over to my 'ouse. Your missus want to talk to 'ee." "Why, my missus is down Ish-peming," said Johnnie. Captain Broad said, "That's all right, but we got one they new telyphones. You come along with me and I'll tell 'ee what to do." So Mr. Rowe went over to Captain Broad's house where there was one of the old-type phones hanging on the wall. Captain Broad said, "Now, Johnnie, stand up against that greaat h'instrument, put your mouth again that pipe and put that 'orn against you ear and say "'Ello!" Johnnie did as di-rected, stood before the phone and said, "'Ello!" Just then the lightning struck the line and knocked him down. He looked at Captain Broad and said, "My Glory, that's the old lady, shore 'nuff!"

THE FOLKSONG

Folksong the world over falls naturally into two parts: narrative and lyric. Narrative songs tell a story; lyric songs, while they may suggest a story, describe an emotion such as love, sorrow, and faith, or form a background to occupational situations. In America, the most important narrative songs are ballads—song-stories of plotted action which use a unique, overlapping scenic technique and which concentrate on the climax so completely that often all motivation and all details leading toward the climax disappear. Ballads in America derive from a British tradition that goes back to medieval times and from the host of sentimental song-stories that were produced in the print shops of the seventeenth-, eighteenth-, and nineteenth-century cities. The more traditional ballads are usually called Child ballads, after Francis James Child, the Harvard professor who edited them in a definitive fashion. The print shop songs are called broadsides, from the sheets on which many of them first appeared. America is rich in both kinds of ballads and has created many similar ones of her own. Then, too, other nations have ballads and some of these songs have been brought to this country. Particularly vigorous is the *corrido* tradition of Mexico and the American Southwest.

Lyric songs, because they center about the expression of emotion, are not easy to classify. Some of them originate from ballads that have lost so much detail that they no longer can be said to tell a story at all. Some center about work rhythms such as the rope-hauling on shipboard or the hammer-swinging of road

gangs. In America, both whites and Negroes developed magnificent spiritual traditions. There are love
lyrics, lyrics to accompany square dances or party
games, lyrics that are nonsense songs and lullabies.
The music halls, political campaigns, labor rallies, and
other such sources have also provided a steady stream
of lyric material, much of which has been picked up
by the folk and made their own. Even to list all the
varied types of American lyric song is quite a task;
perhaps it suffices to indicate that spirituals (both
white and Negro), Negro blues, Spanish love lyrics,
French lyrics, and work songs all offer possibilities so
rich they cry out for investigation.

There are many fine texts and collections to help
those who want to search further into American narrative and lyric folksong. Probably the best guides to
the ballad are the analytical bibliographies published
by the American Folklore Society: G. Malcolm Laws,
Jr.'s *Native American Balladry* (Philadelphia, 1964),
American Balladry from British Broadsides (Philadelphia, 1957), and Tristram P. Coffin's *The British Traditional Ballad in North America* (Philadelphia, 1963).
For a general introduction to both narrative and lyric
traditions, a good book to start with is Alan Lomax's
Folksongs of North America in the English Language
(New York, 1960). From it one can get a general
knowledge of songs of all kinds of ethnic, occupational,
and regional groups; find good bibliographies and dis-
cographies; and learn about the background of many
individual songs.

The Two Sisters

1.

Was two sisters loved one man,
    Jelly flower jan;
    The rose marie;
    The jury hangs o'er
    The rose marie.

2.

He loved the youngest a little the best,
    Jelly flower jan;
    The rose marie;
    The jury hangs o'er
    The rose marie.

3.

Them two sisters going down stream,
    Jelly flower jan;
    The rose marie;
    The jury hangs o'er
    The rose marie.

4.

The oldest pushed the youngest in,
    Jelly flower jan;
    The rose marie;
    The jury hangs o'er
    The rose marie.

5.

She made a fiddle out of her bones,
    Jelly flower jan;
    The rose marie;
    The jury hangs o'er
    The rose marie.

6.

She made the screws out of her fingers,
    Jelly flower jan;
    The rose marie;
    The jury hangs o'er
    The rose marie.

7.

She made the strings out of her hair,
    Jelly flower jan;
    The rose marie;
    The jury hangs o'er
    The rose marie.

8.

The first string says, "Yonder sets my sister on a rock
  Tying of a true-love's knot,"
    Jelly flower jan;
    The rose marie;
    The jury hangs o'er
    The rose marie.

The next string says, "She pushed me in the deep so far."
    Jelly flower jan;
    The rose marie;
    The jury hangs o'er
    The rose marie.

An Indian Love Song

The composer of this song deserted a Ponka woman whom he had courted when he was a youth. He made this song in derision of her. It is sung in two ways: first, as a "song lengthened in singing," and then as a "dancing song."

If it were spoken, it would be thus, two lines representing the reproaches of the woman, and the others the man's reply:

Wisi'çĕ-da^{n'} axa'ge a'çiⁿhe'!	When I think of you, I am weeping as I go!
ḍahe' kĕ a'ahe'-daⁿ axa'ge a'çiⁿhe'!	When I go along the bluffs, I am weeping as I move!
Iⁿçi^{n'}çagece', Nia'giwa'çĕ!	You say that to me, O Niagi-waçe!
Tĕnă'! iɥa^{n'}wiçe-ga^{n'}, i^{n'}pi-ma'ɉi hă.	Fie! as I regard you as my grandmother, I am displeased!

Sung thus:

Wi'-si-çe' ha-xa'-ge ha'-çiⁿ-he' çe'-e-çe+!
Wi'-si-çe' ha-xa'-ge ha'-çiⁿ-he' çe'-e-çe+!
ḍa-he ke'-e ha'-ya-he'-djaⁿ ha-xa'-ge ha'-çiⁿ-he+!
Wi'-si-çe' ha-xa'-ge ha'-çiⁿ-he' çe'-e-çe+!
Hiⁿ-çi^{n'}-ça-ge'-ce+, Ni'-a-gi'-wa-çe, hiⁿ-çi^{n'}-ça-ge'-ce+!
Tĕ-nă'! hi-ɥa^{n'}-wi-çe-gaⁿ+, hiⁿ+-pi-ma-je+! çe'-e-hă'!

When sung as a dancing song, it is in three verses, which, if spoken, would represent the woman and her lover as engaged in a dialogue, thus:

SHE.	*Wisi'çĕ-da^{n'} axa'ge a'taⁿhe'!*	When I think of you, I am weeping as I stand!
	Wisi'çĕ-da^{n'} axa'ge a'taⁿhe'!	
	Wisi'çĕ-da^{n'} axa'ge a'taⁿhe'!	

HE.   *Aⁿça'siçĕ tĕ   I do not think that you re-
          ebçe'gaⁿ-ma'ji hă.*   member me.

SHE.   *Taⁿ'wañgçaⁿ   Yonder remote tribe (vil-
          ga'hiçe'caⁿ*   lage)
        Iça'gi'iñ'ge hĕ.   I do not regard it as of any
                                             value.

        *Çionaⁿ' wi'kaⁿbça   Only you am I desiring as I
          a'taⁿhe'!*   stand!

HE.   *Aⁿça'siçĕ tĕ   I do not think that you re-
          ebçe'gaⁿ-ma'ji hă.*   member me.

HE.   *Ece' ça'ta ce' hă,   You are saying it as you
          Nia'giwa'çĕ!*   stand, O Niagiwaçe!
        Ece' ça'taⁿce' hă.   You are saying it as you
                                             stand.

        *Aⁿça'siça'çĕ tĕ   I do not think that you re-
          ebçe'gaⁿ-ma'ji hă.*   member me.

La Randonnée de la Ville de Paris

1. *C'est dans Paris; | savez-vous c(e) qu'il y a?* (bis)
   Il y a t un(e) ville; | la ville est à Paris.

Refrain.

Jân' Tabricol, savez-vous c(e) qu'il y a?
Mais Jân' Tabricol, savez-vous c(e) qu'il y a?

2. *Mais dans cett(e) ville, | savez-vous c(e) qu'il y a?*
   (bis)
   Il y a t un(e) rue; | la rue est dans la ville;
   La ville est à Paris.

3. *Mais dans cett(e) rue,* | *savez-vous c(e) qu'il y a?*
    (bis)
  Il y at un arbre; | *cet arbre est dans la rue;*
          La rue est dans la ville;
          La ville est à Paris.

4. *Mais dans cet arbre,* | *savez-vous c(e) qu'il y a?*   (bis)
  Il y at un(e) branche; | *la branche est dans l'arbre;*
          L'arbre est dans la rue;
          La rue est dans la ville;
          La ville est à Paris.

5. *Mais dans cett(e) branche,* | *savez-vous c(e) qu'il y a?*
    (bis)
  Il y at un nid; | *le nid est dans la branche;*
          La branche est dans l'arbre;
          L'arbre est dans la rue;
          La rue est dans la ville;
          La ville est à Paris.

6. *Mais dans ce nid,* | *savez-vous c(e) qu'il y a?*   (bis)
  Il y at un œuf; | *cet œuf est dans le nid;*
          Le nid est dans la branche;
          La branche est dans l'arbre;
          L'arbre est dans la rue;
          La rue est dans la ville;
          La ville est dans Paris.

7. *Mais dans cet œuf,* | *savez-vous c(e) qu'il y a?*   (bis)
  Il y at un(e) fille; | *la fille est dans l'œuf;*
          L'œuf est dans le nid;
          Le nid est dans la branche;
          La branche est dans l'arbre;
          L'arbre est dans la rue;
          La rue est dans la ville;
          La ville est à Paris.
    Jân' Tabricol, *savez-vous c(e) qu'il y a?*
    Mais Jân' Tabricol, *savez-vous c(e) qu'il y a?*

TRANSLATION

1. It's in Paris. Do you know what's there?
   There's a town, the town is in Paris.

Refrain: Jân' Tabricol, do you know what's there?
Why Jân' Tabricol, do you know what's there?

2. There's a street; the street is in the town.
3. There's a tree; the tree is on the street.
4. There's a branch; the branch is on the tree.
5. There's a nest; the nest is on the branch.
6. There's an egg; the egg is in the nest.
7. There's a girl; the girl is in the egg.

Trippa, Troppa, Tronjes

Trip - pa, Trop - pa, Tron - jes! De var - kens in de boon - jes, De
ko - jes in de kla - ver, De paar - deen in de ha - ver, De
een - jes in de long - en plass, De goo - jes in de wa - ter plaas, So
[Music here unintelligible]

The pigs are in the beans,
The cows are in the clover,
The horses are in the oats,
The ducks are in the long grass,
The geese are in the water place,
So great my little child is!

Songs for Christmas and the New Year

On New Year's evening as well as on Christmas evening, boys would go from house to house, begging for themselves. One of them carried a bag; and what they collected—fruit, corn, coffee, money, etc.—would be evenly divided among all. On Christmas they sang:

Do natal o redentor 'qui está chegada a função. As sestas feiras vencidas, a minha humilde petição. Nha dá cá, dá cá, nha dá cá face. 'M sa ta ba pa' nin que pouco nha pô na mon. Si nha câ dá, 'm ta mandâ San Jorge ta bem buscâ. Sabe 'ma Jorge é um sant' di bom cunsencia, punde [por ondê] êle entra êle' ta tirá cheo, êle ta dixa pouco.

(From the Saviour's birthday this function came. Fridays overcome, my humble petition. Give here, give here, give here quickly! I will go, however little you put in my hand. If you do not give, I will send St. George to come and look for it. You know that George is a saint of a good conscience; where he enters, he takes out a lot, he leaves little.)

New Year's the boys sing:

San José Sagrada da Maria Angelina, quando foi para Belem rasgatar o menin' de Jesus lá na pé di Santa Crus. Nha dá cá face, nha dá cá face, 'm sa ta ba pa' nin que pouco nha pô na mon. Se nha câ dá, 'Nho' San Jorge ta *rametê. Nossa Senhora fica nesta casa cu' pas' cu' gost' e alegria, alegria pa' tudo mund'.*

(St. José Sagrada da Maria Angelina, when he was at Bethlehem to save a child of Jesus there at the foot of the blessed cross. Give here quickly, give here quickly! I will go, however little you put in my hand. If you do not give, Lord St. George will remit it. [At this point the presents are made, and the boys sing.] May Our Lady be in this house with peace and pleasure and joy, joy for all the world!)

Bands of men as well as of boys go about singing and begging New Year's evening. They sing to the guitar a song almost the same as the song of the boys:

San José Sagrada Maria Angelina, quando foi para Belem rasgatar um minin' di Jesus. San tres pesson Santiximo Trindade. Gaspar Balchor de Butisad'. Nha dá cá face, nha dá cá face. 'M sa ta ba pa' nin que pouco nha pô na mon. Se nha câ dá, 'Nho' San Jorge ta rametê. Nossa Sinhora fica nesta casa cu' paz, cu' gosto, cu' alegria, alegria pa' tudo mund'.

The men also sing,

*Neste dia do Janer', neste dia, dia do Janer', Janero,
É grande mericimento Deus
Por cem Deus ali ofertad', por cem Deus ali ofertad'.
Tambê' sime qui
Christo passa 'strumento.
Tambê' sime qui Christo passa 'strumento.*

(On this day of January, on this day, day of January, January,
Is great merit,
For hundreds [?] God is here offered.
For hundreds God is here offered.
So, too, Christ passed through torment.)

In S. Antão the New Year's evening song of the boys is as follows:

Bendito seja Deus para sempre com grande senhor qui eu ja vi a vossa luz a luz di Deus, sp'rito santo quen da nos lumia na vida e na morte. 'Cordar quem estas adurmido para que lá vem uma trópa reial que para vir dar boas festas do nosso. Queremos a Deus ali na casa do Senhor e Senhora chegam's, homem honrado, que Deus, Nosso Senhor entra dent'o esta casa com gosto e alegria e satisfação e muito serviç' a Deus que hoje é um dia que Deus Nossenhor Jesus Christo foi batisado. O Rei Don

*Jon do Jordon por êle non podia batisar nem no padre,
nem no bispo, nem no arcibispo.*

*Dá cá, dá cá, se o Senhor vae cu me porque já nos
vamos remeter boas festas cu' baptismo do senhor fica
dentro desta casa com alegria, alegria, halelu'a, halelu'a.*

(Blessed be God forever and the great Lord whose light
I saw, the light of God the Holy Ghost, who gives us light
in life and in death. Awake, you who sleep! because there
comes a royal troupe for you to come and give them festive greetings. We ask of God coming here in the house of
Lord and Lady, an honorable man, that God our Lord
enter this house with pleasure and joy and satisfaction and
much service of God, because today is the day that God
our Saviour Jesus Christ was baptized. King Lord John of
Jordan, him no priest could baptize, nor any bishop, nor
any archbishop.

Give here, give here, if the Lord goes with me, because
we are going to bring festive greetings and the baptism of
the Lord to stay in this house with joy, joy, hallelujah,
hallelujah!)

The Ocean Burial

1. "Oh, bury me not in the deep, deep sea!"
   These words came faint and mournfully
   From the pallid lips of a youth who lay
   On his cabin couch, where day by day,
   He had wasted and pined, until o'er his brow,
   The death sweats had slowly passed, and now,
   The scenes of his fondly loved home was nigh,
   And they gathered around him to see him die.

2. "Oh, bury me not in the deep, deep sea,
   Where the billow's shroud shall roll o'er me,
   Where no light can break through the dark, cold wave,
   Or the sun shine sweetly upon my grave!
   Oh, it matters not, I have oft been told,
   Where the body is laid, when the heart grows cold,
   But grant ye, oh, grant ye this boon to me,
   Oh, bury me not in the deep, deep sea!

3. "In fancy I've listened to the well-known words,
   Of the free wild winds and songs of birds,
   I've thought of my home, my cot and bower,
   And the scenes which I loved in my childhood's hour,

Where I've ever hoped to be laid when I died,
In the old churchyard by the green hillside,
Near the home of my father, my grave should be,
Oh, bury me not in the deep, deep sea!

4. "Let my death slumbers be where a mother's prayer
And a sister's tears can be blended there,
For, oh, 't will be sweet, when this heart throb is o'er,
To know, this fountain shall gush no more,
For those who I've earnestly wished for would come,
And plant fresh wild flowers o'er my tomb,
If pleased those loved ones should weep for me,
Oh, bury me not in the deep, deep sea!

5. "And there is another, whose tears might be shed,
For him who lies low in the ocean's bed.
In hours that it pains me to think on now,
She has twined these locks, she has kissed this brow.
The hair she has wreathed will the sea snake hiss,
The heart she has pressed, will wild waves kiss,
For the sake of that loved one who waits for me,
Oh, bury me not in the deep, deep sea!

6. "She has been in my dreams . . ." and his voice failed
there.
And they gave no heed to his dying prayer.
But they lowered him slow o'er the vessel's side,
And above him closed the solemn tide.
Where to dip her wings, the sea fowl rests,
Where the blue waves dash with their foaming crests.
Where the billows do bound, and the wind sports free,
They buried him there in the deep, deep sea!

La Estrella del Norte

Vé-me, vé-me con es-os tus o-jos, Son mas lin-dos que el sol en el cie-lo de que me mi-ran, Me que-dan un con-sue___ lo, Que me ma-ta, que me ma-ta tu mi-rar.

Son tus o-jos la es-trel-la del nor-te,
Que guian en el mar al ma-ri-ne-ro.

Son tus o-jos los o-jos que gui___ an, Y sin el-los no pue-do vi-vir.

Oh, your eyes, dear, your eyes, dear, they pierce me,
As they shine on me, brighter and more potent than the
    sun's rays.
One thought, love, doth console me,
They will kill me, they will kill me, with their flame.
Your eyes are a guide to the mariner,
And constant like rays of the North Star.
Oh, your eyes, love, your eyes, love, they guide me,
For I die, love, I die, without thee.

Ein Stevleik

[The "stev" is] a verse type consisting of four lines, with four beats each, rhymed in couplets, the first couplet having a feminine and the second a masculine rhyme. The ability to compose stanzas of this form was a social accomplishment in Telemark and Setesdal. In these valleys it frequently took the form of poetic debates, in which two persons composed (or recited) alternate stanzas. Such a debate was called a "stevleik," and samples may be found in any collection of Norwegian balladry, or in works such as Aasen's *Ervingen*, which aim to imitate folk life. . . .

It is such a "stevleik" which I wish to present. . . . Further research may possibly reveal the author's name, and the publication date. It is signed H. F. (Hans Foss?), and was printed in a collection of songs published in Chicago in 1894. [Humøret leve! En Samling af Humoristiske Viser, Fædrelands-, Theater-Selskabs- og Drikkesange Tilligemed Et Udvalg af De bedste norske og danske Forfatteres Digte. Illustreret. (Chicago: John Anderson Publishing Co., 1894), pp. 86–88.] The poem presents a debate between one who has been in America a number of years, and is accordingly well-satisfied with his country, and one who has just arrived from Norway, still nostalgic for his home, and antagonistic to the new conditions in America. The author gives the newcomer the last word, and seems to sympathize with his pessimistic views. But both sides are well presented, and the whole ballad testifies to the skill and poetic talents of its author.

Nykomargut

No er eg hugad, no vil eg
    kveda,
Med andre glade eg vil meg
    gleda.
Med ulveflokken eg er ilag,
Eg skal no tute den heile
    dag.

Norsk-Amerikaner

Ja glad, det kan du vel sag-
    tens vera,
Som slap i Noreg paa posen
    bera.
No slepp du kravle i berg
    og ur
Og plage øyret med fosse-
    dur.

Nykomargut

Javist, der rørde du ved dei
    strengjir,
Som drev or heimen so
    mange drengjir.
Den nye tid med si fram-
    skridtsand
Hev liten vyrdnad for heim
    og land.

Norsk-Amerikaner

Det høyrest snodigt, naar
    slike talar
Um vyrdnad, framskridt og
    heimsens dalar,
Som ikkje eigde en fod med
    jord
I draumelandi der langt
    mod nord.

Newcomer Boy

Tonight I'm in good spirits,
now I want to sing and
make merry with others.
All day long I have to run
around and howl with the
rest of the wolves.

Norwegian-American

Yes, you have reason to be
merry, for now you'll never
have to bear the poor man's
lot in Norway. You'll never
have to pick your way 'mid
rock and precipice, or en-
dure again the rumbling of
the waterfalls.

Newcomer Boy

Yes, to be sure, there you
touched the strings that
drove so many lads from
home. Our modern age
with its spirit of progress
has so little respect for
home and native land.

Norwegian-American

It sounds odd to hear fellows like you talk about respect, and progress, and the
valleys of home, you who
didn't own a foot of ground
in the dream land of the
North.

Nykomargut

Nei, brev og sjøte eg aldrig
aatte
Paa gardelutar med skog og
slotte,
Men heile landet laag frisk
og frit,
Og alt tilsamman eg kallad
mit.

Newcomer Boy

No, it's true I had no deeds
or documents to show my
ownership of farms and
manors. But the whole
country lay fresh and free
before me, and I called all
of it mine.

Norsk-Amerikaner

Men skulde du deg som
andre klare,
Du fik vist ikkje kring landi
fare.
Tænk heile sumaren stande
slaa
Framyver bøygd med en
stuttorvljaa.

Norwegian-American

But you didn't get much
chance to travel around and
look at it, if you were going to make a decent living.
Just think of having to
stand all summer bent forward over a short-handled
scythe!

Nykomargut

Du skulde vist, ho var rar,
den tidi,
Der uppaa sætrane under
lidi;
Somangei løgje daa vinden
bar,
Fraa ragstegjente til slaat-
tekar.

Newcomer Boy

You should have known
what rare experiences they
were, those summer days
on the mountain heights.
So many a jest was bandied
back and forth from boy to
girl, while they worked at
their haying.

Norsk-Amerikaner

Retso, no er du paa isen
haale;
Jau, jentun dikkans, dei var
nok snaale;
Tænk, vadmaalsstakken av
spunnen traa,
Det var vel syn, som var
værdt at sjaa.

Norwegian-American

Indeed, now you're skating
on thin ice, talking about
those wonderful girls in
Norway! What sights they
must have been, in their
coarse homespun skirts!

Nykomargut

Nei, gled deg du i dei fine
    blanke.
Eg hever sannspurgt, der
    tidt kan banke
Eit bedre hjarte, der armod
    grin,
Held der, som gullet aa
    silkje sjin.

Newcomer Boy

You are welcome to enjoy
your pretty little dolls! I
know it for a fact that often
a better heart may beat
amid the starkest poverty
than in glittering gold and
silks.

Norsk-Amerikaner

Aa stakkars gut, du bleiv
    hardt bedregjen,
Som tok i skunndingen
    denne vegen.
Her hev me bruk for din
    spræke arm,
Kon skjel det eit du er kold
    held varm.

Norwegian-American

Poor boy, you were badly
fooled when you all too
hastily set out upon this
course. Here we have use
for your trusty arm, but
care not a bit whether you
are warm or cold.

Nykomargut

Tak skal du hava for desse
    ordi!
Ein lærer altid litt her paa
    jordi;
Den læra hev eg no pren-
    tad meg,
I Noreg var eg mest lukke-
    leg.

Newcomer Boy

I thank you for these words
of yours! One can always
learn something every-
where in this world; and
the thing I have learned for
sure is that in Norway I
had the greater happiness.

Ten Thousand Miles Away

No more recalled. *Chorus.*

1. Oh! my true love, she was handsome,
    And my true love, she was young;
  Her eyes were blue as the violet's hue,
    And silvery was the sound of her tongue.
  And silvery was the sound of her tongue, my boys;
    But while I sing this lay-ay-ay,
  She has taken a trip in a government-ship,
    Ten thousand miles away.

Chorus.
  Then blow, ye winds, heigh-ho!
    A-roving I will go;
  I'll stay no more on England's shore,
    But let the music play-ay-ay,
  For I'm off on the morning train,
    Across the raging main,
  For I'm on my way to my own true love,
    Ten thousand miles away.

2. The sun may shine through an eastern fog,
    The Hudson run bright and clear,
  The ocean's brine be turned to wine,
    And I forget my beer,
  And I forget my beer, my boys,
    In the landlord's quarts lay-ay-ay;
  But I never will part from my own sweetheart,
    Ten thousand miles away.

3. Oh! dark and dismal was the day
    When last I saw my Meg,
  She'd a government band around each hand,
    And another one round her leg,
  And another one round her leg, my boys;
    But while I sing this lay-ay-ay,
  She has taken a trip in a government-ship,
    Ten thousand miles away.

Pig in the Parlor

|: We've got a new pig in the parlor, :| [three times]
|: And he is Irish too. :| [three times]

Chorus.

The right hand to your partner,
The left hand to your neighbor;
Then pass right through to the next we meet,
And we'll all promenade.

We'll all promenade,
We'll all promenade;
We'll pass right through to the next we meet,
And we'll all promenade.

I've a Long Time Heard

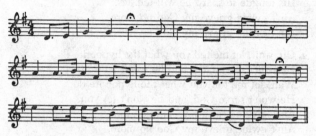

I've a long time heard the sun will be bleeding,
  The sun will be bleeding, the sun will be bleeding,
I've a long time heard the sun will be bleeding:
  Sinner, where will you stand in that day?

I've a long time heard the angels will be singing, etc.

I've a long time heard the devils will be howling, etc.

I've a long time heard sinners would be crying, etc.

Ain't Gwine Grieve My God No More

1. Hypocrite, hypocrite, God despise,
   His tongue so sharp he will tell lies;
   Hypocrite, hypocrite, God despise,
   His tongue so sharp he will tell lies.
   Ain't gwine grieve my God no more,
   Ain't gwine grieve my God no more.

2. Oh, wait, let me tell you what the hypocrite do,
   He won't serve God, and he won't let you;
   Wait, let me tell you what the hypocrite do,
   He won't serve God, and he won't let you.
   Ain't gwine grieve my God no more,
   Ain't gwine grieve my God no more.

3. Stop, let me tell you what the hypocrite do,
   He won't go to heaven, and he won't let you;
   Stop, let me tell you what the hypocrite do,
   He won't go to heaven, and he won't let you.
   Ain't gwine grieve my God no more,
   Ain't gwine grieve my God no more.

4. Oh, if I had died the day when I was young,
   I would not had this troubled race to run;
   Oh, if I had died the day when I was young,
   I would not had this troubled race to run.
   Ain't gwine grieve my God no more,
   Ain't gwine grieve my God no more.

5. If you want to get to heaven, let me tell you how,
   Treat your neighbor like you ought to right here now;
   If you want to get to heaven, let me tell you how,
   Treat your neighbor like you ought to right here now.
   Ain't gwine grieve my God no more,
   Ain't gwine grieve my God no more.

6. I don't want to stumble, I don't want to fall,
   I want to get to heaven when the roll is called;
   I don't want to stumble, I don't want to fall,
   I want to get to heaven when the roll is called.
   Ain't gwine grieve my God no more,
   Ain't gwine grieve my God no more.

7. The Old Satan is mad, and I am glad,
   And he missed that soul he thought he had;
   The Old Satan is mad, and I am glad,
   And he missed that soul he thought he had.
   Ain't gwine grieve my God no more,
   Ain't gwine grieve my God no more.

8. The Old Satan have him in a tight compress,
   When the bugle blow he change his dress;
   The Old Satan have him in a tight compress,
   When the bugle blow he change his dress.
   Ain't gwine grieve my God no more,
   Ain't gwine grieve my God no more.

9. The Old Satan wear an iron shoe,
   If you don't mind, he gwine step on you;
   The Old Satan wear an iron shoe,
   If you don't mind he gwine step on you.
   Ain't gwine grieve my God no more,
   Ain't gwine grieve my God no more.

10. The Old Satan is a liar and a conger too,
    If you don't mind he gwine conger you;
    The Old Satan is a liar and a conger too,
    If you don't mind he gwine conger you.
    Ain't gwine grieve my God no more,
    Ain't gwine grieve my God no more.

11. When I was walking down in dead men's lane,
    Wrapt and tired in my sin and shame,
    When I was walking down in dead men's lane,
    Wrapt and tired in my sin and shame,

Ain't gwine grieve my God no more,
Ain't gwine grieve my God no more.

12. The very hour I thought I was lost,
My dungeon shook and my chains fell off;
The very hour I thought I was lost,
My dungeon shook and my chains fell off.
Ain't gwine grieve my God no more,
Ain't gwine grieve my God no more.

Railroad Blues

Every time you hear me sing this song
You may know I've caught a train and gone.
I get a letter, and this is how it read:
Stamped on the inside, "Yo lover's sick in bed."

Give me my shoes and my Carhart overalls,
Let me step over yonder and blind the Cannon Ball;
That's the long train they call the Cannon Ball,
It makes a hundred miles and do no switchin' at all.

Train I ride doan burn no coal at all,
It doan burn nothin' but Texas Beaumont oil;
That's the long train they calls the Cannon Ball,
It makes a hundred miles and do no stoppin' at all.

If you ever had the blues, you know jus' how I feel,
Puts you on the wonder, and make you want to squeal;
When you take the blues and doan know what to do,
Jus' hunt you a train and ride the whole world through.

Big Four in Dallas done burned down,
Burned all night long, burned clean to the ground;
But give me my shoes, and press my overalls,
If you doan min' my goin', baby, I'll catch the Cannon Ball.

I'm worried now, but I won't be worried long,
This northbound train will certainly take me home.
Number Nine is gone, Number Ten's switchin' in the yard,
But I'm goin' to see that girl if I have to ride the rods.

I got the railroad blues, but I haven't got the fare,
The company sho' ought to pay my way back there.
The train I ride is sixteen coaches long
Dat's de train done take yo' baby home.

I'm a goin' away, it won't be long;
When I hit Houston, I'll call it gone.
When I git to Houston I'll stop and dry;
When I hit San Tone, I'll keep on by.

How I hate to hear the monkey motion blow,
It puts me on the wonder, and makes we want to go.
Dat passenger train got ways jus' lak a man,
Steal away yo' girl, and doan care where she land.

I may be right an' I may be wrong,
But it takes a worried woman to sing a worry song;
When a woman's in trouble, she wring her hands and cry;
But when a man's in trouble, it's a long freight train and
   ride.

Lob-Gesang

The special claim of the Amish to the interest of the
folklorist rests on several points. First, the Amish have preserved a simple sixteenth-century German peasant tradition in the midst of our complex American society. In
dress, in manners, in folk ways, in language, in forms of
religious worship, they still preserve the tradition of the
respectable Christian peasant farmer of the German Pala-
tinate, of Alsace-Lorraine, and of colonial Pennsylvania.
Second, they use the sixteenth-century German hymnal,

containing hymns composed by their martyr forefathers in the best sixteenth-century German folk-poetry tradition. And third, they still sing those hymns to the same tunes to which their Swiss Brethren forebears sang them over four centuries ago.

. . . The . . . tune printed below was notated by Mr. Arthur W. Roth, who became familiar with a number of the Amish tunes by attending Amish church services in southeastern Iowa. This hymn, called by the Amish the *Lob-Gesang,* is sung as the second hymn in every Amish church service in America. This hymn, Number 131 on page 770 of the *Ausbund,* is one of the shorter hymns, having only four seven-line stanzas. Mr. Roth states that pages of explanation would be necessary to instruct anyone in singing the hymns as the Amish sing them. No one, he says, has yet written these tunes in conventional music score and even if it were possible to do so, it would be impossible to teach anyone to reproduce their tone and spirit accurately. The Amish sing them with a depth of sincerity, a feeling of true Christian piety difficult to imitate.

Herr _____ gna-dig - - - - - lich, An _____

uns _____ neu _____ hast _____ be - wie - -

sen, Und _____ hast _____ uns _____ Herr _____

zu - - sam - men _____ g'führt, Uns _____

zu _____ er - - - mah - - nen _____ durch _____

Dein _____ Wort. Gieb _____ uns _____

Ge - - - nad _____ zu _____ die _____ sem.

TRANSLATION

O God, Father, we glorify Thee, and praise Thy good-
ness, that Thou hast,

O Lord, graciously manifested Thyself anew to us, and
hast brought us together,

Lord, to admonish us through Thy word. Give us grace
for this.

The Death of the Beckwith Child

A SHORT ACCOUNT OF THE AWFULL & SURPRISING DETH OF
THE CHILD OF DANIEL & SARAH BECKWITH, WHO DE-
PARTED THIS LIFE JUNE YE 20TH DAY, AD, 1773.

1. my frends allow my febel toungue,
   if I may speak my mind,
   this plainly shoes to old and young
   the frailty of mankind

2. the child that in the wods retiar
   is lost while parants moarn,
   and othars are consumd by fiar
   or into peses toarn.

3. permit my febel pen to rite
   what has ben laitly dun,
   a man who plast his cheaf delight
   in his beloved son.

4. in manchester whare he ingoys
   provision for this life,
   he had two dafters and three boys
   by his beloved wife.

5. his second son, robbens by name,
   was ten years old and moar,
   on him this sad distruction came,
   who was in peses toar.

6. the fathar said, my children thair
   if you will clear sum land,
   you shall posess all it doth bair
   to be at your command.

7. the parants then did both agree,
   to tinmouth took their way,
   a moarning sister for to see,
   but long they did not stay.

8. the prity boys, wee understand,
   did lovingly agree
   all for to clear the peas of land
   set fiar to a tree.

9. the chunk was thirty feat in length
   and was exceding dry,
   so rotten it had not much strength
   did burn most vemantly.

10. the boys against a log did lean
    or on it setting all,
    and nothing was for to be seen
    untill the tree did fall.

11. but oh, alass, the dismall blow
    struck robbens to the ground,
    his head was masht two peses soo,
    a deep and deadly wound.

12. his head and arms all broke to bits,
    he in the fiar did lye,
    the children scard out of their wits
    aloud began two cry.

13. the elder son that yet remains,
    resevd a grevous wound,
    but oh, alass, poor robbens brains
    did fall out on the ground.

14. thus he within the flame did lye,
    the othars full of greaf,
    a neighbor that did hear them cry
    did run to their releaf.

15. this maid his tendar hart to ake
    to see him in that case;
    he quickly hold on him did take
    and drue him from that place.

16. now near the middel of the day
    the neighbors thay did meat,
    the corps thay quickly did convay
    in to his winding sheat.

17. a frend to tinmouth took his coast
    the hevey news to beair.
    the tidings come to them all most
    as soon as thay got their.

18. but when the parants come two know
    theair son was dead indeed,
    alass, their eys with tears did flow
    and homwards went with spead.

19. the peopel came from every part
    to see the awfull sight,
    it grevd the parants tender hart,
    alass, and well it might.

20. to see their one beloved son
    in such a case indeed,
    me thinks would make a hart of stone
    or hart of steall to blead.

21. laid in the grave two turn to dust,
    their greaf what tongue can tell,
    but yet, alass, the parants must
    bid him a long fair well

Asesinato de Francisco Villa

acaecida en Parral, Chihuahua, el 19 de Julio de 1923.

Villa, doquiera que te
   halles
De esa región escondida,
Si ignoras quien de tu vida
Cortó sus tremendos ayes;
Vale mas, Pancho, que
   calles,
Porque aunq' el asunto es
   serio
Para nadie es un misterio
Que en materia de elección
Externaste tu opinión,
Que te llevó al Cementerio.

   Por los pueblos y ciu-
      dades,
Por las Plazas y las Calles,
Por las llanuras y valles,
Se cuentan atrocidades.
¿Cuáles serán las verdades
O el motivo de tu muerte?
Por hombre, tu ingrata
   suerte
Te llevó hasta "Canutillo"
Y cual manso pajarillo . . .
¡Adiós, Pancho; hasta más
   verte!

   Tu mala estrella lo
      quiere,
(Que no fué del todo in-
   grata)

Por lo que: el que a fierro
   mata,
Se ha dicho que a fierro
   muere.
Y aquel que mal hiciere
Su conciencia lo atormenta
Y hay qué tener en cuenta
Que fuistes un criminal
Que a todos hiciste mal
Y ante el mundo eras
   afrenta.

   Tú, con tu poder y tu oro
Y tu escolta de "Dorados,"
Gozaban, pero enjaulados
La libertad, con desdoro.
De tus crímenes en coro
El mundo los repetía
Esperando siempre el día
De que tu afán se acabara
Y tu vida liquidara
Tanta infamia y felonía.

   Son inútiles los ¡ayes!
Y demás inculpaciones
Porque, Villa, tus acciones,
Corrieron montes y valles.
Ahora, sea Enríquez o
   Calles,
Chao, o cualquiera ene-
   migo,
Todo mundo es un testigo

Que por criminal eterno
Te dió un gran premio el
    Gobierno
Como al más honrado
    amigo.

  Deja, al fin, que satisfaga
La justicia su sentencia,
Es ley de la Providencia:
Lo que se debe, se paga.
Si tú clabaste tu daga
En niños y hasta en an-
    cianos,
En hermanos y no her-
    manos
Porque el crimen te empu-
    jaba,
México se sonrojaba
Por tus actos inhumanos.

  De Villa el asesinato
Aun no se puede aclarar

Ni se han podido atrapar
Los que lo echaron al plato.
Todo se ha vuelto alegato
Ahora que Villa cayó;
Pero si Pancho murió
Ya no habrá temores más
De que se altere la paz,
Porque Villa, ya perdió.
  Ahora el asunto es
    sencillo:

De cordura dando un rasgo,
Si se acabó el compadrazgo,
Recójase "Canutillo."
El Gobierno, dando brillo
A la Ley y la Justicia,
Reparta entre la milicia
Todo el material de guerra
Y repártase la tierra
Sin ventajas ni avaricia.

TRANSLATION

Assassination of Francisco Villa

occurred at Parral, Chihuahua, July 19, 1923

Villa, wherever you are,
Whatever the place may be,
If you do not know the cause
Of your life's last agony,
Pancho, you'd better not ask,
Because the affair, though serious,
Is to none a mystery;
For in political strife
You had made your choices known,
And it has cost you your life.

In the towns and in the cities,
In the squares and in the streets,
Over the plains and the valleys
There were tales of your misdeeds;
We are not sure of the truth
Or the reason for your death;
Cruel fate rewarded you
With the lands of "Canutillo" [Villa's hacienda]
And there, like a little bird . . .
Goodbye, Pancho, till we see you!

Your destiny wished it so
(Though once it had been your friend),
But he who lives by the sword
By the sword as well must end;
And he who does wrong to others
With his conscience must contend;
Well we remember the crimes
That were coupled to your name,
You did wrong to everyone
And brought your country to shame.

Surrounded by your "Dorados" [bodyguard]
In wealth and power you raged,
You tarnished the face of freedom
And lived like a beast uncaged;
The world repeated in chorus
All of your barbarous ways,
And hoped that your rage would lessen
And looked forward to the time
When your death would bring an end
To such felony and crime.

All accusations are useless,
All lamentation and woe,
For, Villa, your evil deeds
Through hills and valleys did go;
Was it Enríquez or Calles,
Chao, or some other foe?
The world itself can bear witness
That for your crimes without end
You were handsomely rewarded
Like the government's best friend.

Let there be justice at last
And its verdict satisfy,
For such is the law of God:
The doer of wrong must die;
Yes, for your dagger was plunged
Into children and the old,
Into Mexican and stranger,
For such was the life you led;
And for these inhuman acts
All Mexico bowed its head.

As for finding out who did it,
No one knows where to begin,
And they have not apprehended
The people who "did him in";
Everyone is making charges,

There is much squabbling and din;
But now that Pancho is dead
Things are no longer the same,
The peace will not be disturbed
For Villa has lost the game.

And now the matter is simple,
Let's take a sensible stand,
No more of deals and backscratching
And recover Villa's land;
Thus the government may honor
Both justice and law as planned;
Give his weapons to the army,
Each according to his need,
And let the land be divided
Without crookedness or greed.

Silver Jack

I was on the Drive in eighty,
    Working under Silver Jack,
Which the same was now in Jackson
    And ain't soon expected back.
And there was a fellow 'mongst us
    By the name of Robert Waite
Kind of cute and smart and tonguey,
    Guess he was a graduate.

He could talk on any subject,
    From the Bible down to Hoyle,
And his words flowed out so easy,
    Just as smooth and slick as oil.
He was what they call a sceptic,
    And he loved to sit and weave
Hifalutin words together
    Telling what he didn't believe.

One day we all were sittin' round
   Waiting for a flood, smoking Nigger-head tobacco,
And hearing Bob expound.
   Hell, he said, was all a humbug,
And he made it plain as day
   That the Bible was a fable;
And we 'lowed it looked that way.
   Miracles and such like
Were too rank for him to stand;
   And as for him they called the Saviour,
He was just a common man.

"You're a liar!" some one shouted,
   "And you've got to take it back."
Then everybody started—
   'Twas the words of Silver Jack.
And he cracked his fists together
   And he stacked his duds and cried,
"'Twas in that thar religion
   That my mother lived and died;
And though I haven't always
   Used the Lord exactly right,
Yet when I hear a chump abuse him
   He must eat his words or fight."

Now, this Bob he weren't no coward,
   And he answered bold and free,
"Stack your duds and cut your capers,
   For there ain't no flies on me."
And they fit for forty minutes,
   And the crowd would whoop and cheer
When Jack spit up a tooth or two,
   Or when Bobby lost an ear.

But at last Jack got him under
   And he slugged him onct or twist,
And straightway Bob admitted
   The divinity of Christ.

But Jack kept reasoning with him
    Till the poor cuss gave a yell,
And 'lowed he'd been mistaken
    In his views concerning hell.

Then the fierce encounter ended
    And they riz up from the ground,
And some one brought a bottle out
    And kindly passed it round.
And we drank to Bob's religion
    In a cheerful sort o'way,
But the spread of infidelity
    Was checked in camp that day.

I'm a Good Old Rebel

1. I served with old Bob Lee three years about,
    Got wounded in four places, and starved at Point Lookout.
    I caught the rheumatism camping in the snow.
    I killed a sight of Yankees, and wish I'd killed some more.

Chorus:
    For I'm a good old rebel, that's what I am,
    And for this land of freedom I don't care a damn.
    I'm glad I fought against her; I only wish we'd won,
    And I don't ask no pardons for anything I've done.

2. I hate the Constitution, the great Republic too;
    I hate the mighty eagle and the uniform of blue;
    I hate the glorious banner and all their flags and fuss;
    Those lying, thieving Yankees, I hate 'em wuss and wuss.

3. I won't be reconstructed, I'm better now than them;
    For those dirty carpetbaggers I don't give a damn.
    So I'm off to the border as soon as I can go;
    I'll get me a gun and leave for Mexico.

Bishop Zack

Zack Black came to Utah back in Eighty-Three,
A right good Mormon and a Bishop, too, was he,
He ran a locomotive on the "D'n' R. G.,"
And Zack was awful popular as you will see.

Chorus
    Hear him whistle!
    He ran a locomotive on the "D'n' R. G."

Zack he had a wife in every town,
He numbered them from twelve 'way down to number
    two,
Oh, in his locomotive he'd go steaming 'round,
And when he'd pass each wifie's home his whistle blew.

Zack he always said he loved 'em all the same,
But wifie number twelve he loved her mighty well,
He had her picture mounted in his engine cab,
And when he passed her home he'd always ring the bell.

Listen ev'rybody, 'cause this story's true,
Zack had a wife in ev'ry town his train passed through.
They tried to shift Zack over to the old "U. P.,"
But Zack demurred, 'cause he preferred the "D'n' R. G."

Sellin' That Stuff

Aunt Jane had a dance and she had a crowd,
She sold more whisky than the law allowed;
She's sellin' that stuff,
Aunt Jane, she's sellin' that stuff,
She can really break the record
When it comes to sellin' that stuff.

Aunt Jane stayed out all night long,
She didn't come home till the break of dawn,
She's sellin' that stuff,
She can really break that record
When it comes to sellin' that stuff.

Took Aunt Jane to the county jail,
She didn't need anybody to go her bail,
She's sellin' that stuff.

She sold some corn and she sold some gin,
She sold it to the women and she sold it to the men.
She's still sellin' that stuff,
She's still sellin' that stuff.

Uncle Jim went to jail with a heavy load,
They give him thirty days on the county road
For buyin' that stuff.
He can really break the record when it comes to buyin'
    that stuff.

Aunt Jane got a sister and her name is Lil,
She used to sell that stuff and she's sellin' it still,
That's sellin' that stuff, that's sellin' that stuff,
That really break the record when it comes to sellin' that
    stuff.
Sell that stuff! Sell that stuff!
She can really break the record when it comes to sellin'
    that stuff.

McKinley and Huey Long

McKinley

McKin-ley— went to Buf-fa-lo, thought he knew it all.
Was-n't— long be-fore he was land-ed with a
ball, Ain't it— sad. Rush him to the
hos-pi-tal, Lay him— on the stand Mc-Kin-ley says to
doc-tor, Won't— you save me if you can. etc.

1. McKinley went to Buffalo, thought he knew it all
   Wasn't long before he was landed with a ball
   Ain't it sad.

2. Rush him to the hospital, lay him on the stand
   McKinley says to doctor, "Won't you save me if you
   can."
   Ain't it sad.

3. People in the hospital all gather 'round
   McKinley says to doctor, "Won't you please lay me
   down."
   Aint it sad.

HUEY LONG

M.m. ♩= 176.

Hu - ey be - gan to hol - la, Hu - ey be - gan to squall,
says to the Doc - tor, bet you can't find that ball. An' I'm
gone.— Lawd knows I'm gone. It was too bad——
Hu - ey had to go. For he'd ta - ken— from the rich— and he'd
giv - en— to the poor, ain't it sad?—— Lawd knows it's sad.

1. Oh Huey Long was a good old man
   But he had to go when he can,
   Ain't it sad, Lawd knows it's sad.

   Refrain:
   It was too bad Huey had to go.
   For he'd taken from the rich
   And he'd given to the poor,
   Ain't it sad? Lawd knows it's sad.

2. Taken him to that hospital,
   Laid him on that stand.
   Huey says to the Doctor,
   "Won't you save me if you can?"
             Refrain.

3. Huey began to holla,
   Huey began to squall.
   Says to the Doctor, "Bet you can't find that ball.
   "An' I'm gone, Lawd knows I'm gone."
   Refrain.

4. It was too bad Huey had to go.
   For he'd taken from the rich and he'd given to the poor.
   Refrain.

5. People in the hospital all gather 'round.
   Huey says to the Doctor, "Won't you please lay me
   down."
   Refrain.

6. Huey's wife gazed in his face,
   Says, "I'm sorry. Sorry that I can't take your place."
   Refrain.

7. With a steel tire buggy an' a rubber tire hack,
   Taken him to that cemetery an' refused to bring him
   back.
   Refrain.

8. Guy shot Huey, taken a chance to run.
   Marched him 'round Louisiana and cut him down with
   a gun.
   Refrain.

The Haunted Wood

(♩=50)

Rug - ged rocks well they had ris - en___ Far up -
on on ev - 'ry side, A migh-ty ba - sin had been
washed there by a ma - ny a com - ing tide.

2. On the banks there lived a white man,
   Wife and children he had three,
   While the winds were softly sighing
   And a-moaning through the trees.

3. On the bosom of this river
   Launched a many a light canoe,
   While the winds were softly sighing
   And the summer skies were blue.

4. While this busy little father
   To the town for mail had gone,
   Left his wife and little children
   For a few short hours alone.

5. There this busy little mother
   Had no time for thought of fear,
   While the winds were softly sighing
   And the summer skies were clear.

6. Hark! She hears the tramp of horses.
   It was then she turned in fright
   Just in time to draw the door bolt
   As the Indians rode in sight.

7. Then she seized and kissed her babies,
   Bid them neither speak or cry,
   Locked them in a secret closet
   And she knelt herself to die.

8. Then in anger broke the chieftain,
   Tore the bolt from off the door,
   There they found the weeping woman
   Lying there upon the floor.

9. Then they danced and sang around her
   Heeding not her piteous cries,
   Grabbed her by her dark brown tresses,
   Her screams of gloom reached to the skies.

10. Then she begged and cried for mercy
    As she knelt upon the floor,
    While they danced and sang around her,
    Then they dragged her through the door.

11. 'Mid frenzied glee, their war cries swelling,
    It was then they gathered 'round,
    Then they burned the little dwelling
    With the babies to the ground.

12. Now the old man wanders lonely
    'Round the place where the dwelling stood,
    And the people of the village
    Call the place the Haunted Wood.

se below which point out the stupidity of an un-
ar candidate, condemn an unfavored nominee, and
ze a favorite.

Duke Kahanamoku,
The champion of
Oahu.
Duke Kahanamoku,
The swimmer of the
islands.
Duke Kahanamoku,
He swam to Los An-
geles,
And now he's pump-
ing gasoline.

You vote for mayor
Crane;
You eat mountain ap-
ple.
You vote for mayor
Petrie;
You chew sugar cane.
You vote for Ichinose,
Muscles on the body,
Superman for super-
visor.

(11) You vote for Tommy
Lee;
He makes you go on
a spree.
You vote for Bobby
Lee;
He gives you all the
whiskey.
You vote for Herbert
Lee,
And then you will see
The very end of
democracy.

(12) Lester Petrie,
He runs the town.
The local graft
Is now going down.
He runs the town
To perfection,
So give him your vote
bull, next election!

Rhymes from Hawaii

These verses were sung in Hawaii before, during, and
after World War II. . . . All of the verses collected were
sung to the same melody. They exhibit a high degree of
formal variation and little adherence to rhyme pattern.
Collectively, they are known as "Lei Ana Ika" or
"U.S.E.D." The origin of the melody is unknown but, according to informants, the first words appeared just before
the war.

The most common, and reportedly the oldest of these
verses, was developed shortly before World War II. It
describes some of the widespread hostility which was ex-
pressed toward the United States Engineers Department
before and during the war. The U.S.E.D. was famous
for its arbitrary actions and its inefficiency. However, it
employed large numbers of island men on construction
projects, and this verse was sung by the men en route to
and from work each day:

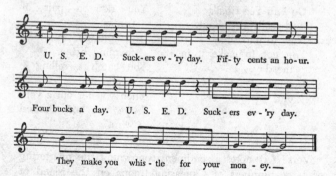

U. S. E. D. Suck-ers ev-'ry day. Fif-ty cents an ho-ur.

Four bucks a day. U. S. E. D. Suck-ers ev-'ry day.

They make you whis-tle for your mon-ey.

When the war started the song gained currency. New
verses were composed and sung at beach parties, drink-

ing parties, *luaus*—wherever people got together. One informant described their popularity thus: "'Lei Ana Ika,' as far as I know, had no set or one singer or writer. It was more like a folksong. At every party someone would start the first verse and then each person in turn would add a verse—maybe a new one he had thought up, or an old one. The verses usually fit in with the party, or something new that had happened in the war effort, or change in politics."

In the following, which are typical of verses that emerged during the war years, (2) is a protest against the blackout. ("Lau Yee Chai's" refers to a popular restaurant in Honolulu; "Lei ana ika" is apparently a nonsense phrase used to keep the meter.) Verse (3) has reference to the barbed wire on the beaches. (Makapuu is a beach on Oahu; the phrase "Awe na hoi" is an expression of pain.)

(2) Before time
At night you could go
out.
Go Lau Yee Chai's
And really get about.
Now to make hay
You got to make it in
the day.
Lei ana ika, the blackout!

(3) Body surfing at Makapuu
Used to be very fine.
You don a pair of
trunks
And plunge into the
foaming brine.
You catch a rolling
swell
Then you let out a yell,
"Awe na hoi! Barbed
wire!"

Verse (4) notes a sentiment concerning the quartering of large numbers of Caucasian troops on the island of Hawaii, while (5) ridicules the spy scare. ("Baby donkey" is slang for half caste.)

(4) The marines landed
In Kailua Bay.
The girls go crazy
About what they say.
Nine months later
They feel the pain,
Lei ana ika, baby donkey.

(5) Took m
For a b
The me
Up so
Step on
The jalo
Lei ana

in th
popu
eulo

(9

Verse (6) satirizes tire rationing; verse
are two of several which comment on the
in downtown Honolulu during the war.
"makai" are opposite directions; the line '
eye" refers to going blind; "Holo holo" n
H.R.T. stands for Honolulu Rapid Transit.)

(6) I went down town
To buy a car.
I went down town
To buy a Ford V8.
I step on the gas,
Four tires flat.
Lei ana ika, tire ration.

(7) Before time
When you go to town,
You could go Bethel
Street
And go all around,

But now
town
The cop he
"Open you
only one

(8) Fort Street
Now makai.
Go so many
Make pia th
You can tak
But not for
I holo holo
H.R.T.

(10

Some verses were concerned with public
popular one ridiculed a territorial hero, Duk
moku, a former Olympic swimmer, who temp
came a rather unpopular figure as the director
rationing during the war. Other verses cham
vored political candidates or ridiculed the opp

The Dehorn Song

The dehorn's nose is deepest red,
The one bright spot on his empty head.
To get his booze he begs and steals,
Half-naked he goes without his meals.

Chorus
Oh dehorn, why don't you get wise,
And quit the booze and organize?
A sober mind will win the day,
The One Big Union will show the way.

And when the dehorn gets a job,
He's satisfied, the dirty slob.
A pile of straw will do for a bed
On which to rest his wooden head.

To stick around and fix the job,
It never pierced his empty nob.
For fifty cents will get him drunk,
And fifty cents a lousy bunk.

And when the dehorn gets stakebound,
He starts to dream about the town.
He kicks about the rotten chuck,
And never saw such a sticky muck.

Oh point to him with nose so red
With tangled feet and soggy head.
For all this life to him will yield
Is just a grave in potter's field.

SUPERSTITIONS

Should someone steal oil of baptism from a Roman Catholic church in order to combat witchcraft, would this act be religious or superstitious? The answer will depend entirely on the outlook of the person replying to the question, for superstitions seem to be simply those beliefs which lie outside the particular faith of the person making the definition.

Superstitions can be divided into two general groups: those handed down by the culture as a whole (the bad luck associated with black cats, the number thirteen, the broken mirror, walking under a ladder); and those developed by each individual out of his own fortunes and misfortunes (the refusal of the athlete to shave before a big game, the desire of the actress to wear a certain ring during each performance). Even in a highly sophisticated society, everyone cherishes a few superstitions of both kinds, for although they are associated in most people's minds with backwardness, irrationality, and forgotten magic, most of us do not like to flout them completely. And it isn't particularly relevant whether or not they really work. Weather beliefs that do work for Yorkshire, England, may be stubbornly asserted in Maine, Iowa, California, where they have been carried by succeeding generations and where they have no validity in the new climate.

Because they are so idiosyncratic and so personal, superstitions are extremely hard to trace. There is no good general study of them, although Wayland D. Hand, who has been attempting to catalogue American beliefs for over twenty years, has written a definitive essay in Volume VI of the *Frank C. Brown Collection of North Carolina Folklore* (Durham, N. C., 1961). One can also turn with profit to a study of a particular superstition such as Evon Z. Vogt and Ray Hyman's classic, *Water Witching, U.S.A.* (Chicago, 1959).

To Charm Cattle and Cure Injuries

The following charm, from Oulu in Finland and Crooked Lake in Minnesota, was used to make cows come home from the wild pastures, when they were first let out in the spring. Salt from a bell was fed to the cow leading the herd, then the bell was fastened to its neck, and the *loihtija* [wise woman] chanted:

Kellon kaulahan sivallan	I lash the bell to the neck
Kuulun kellon lehmälleni	The well-known bell for my cow.
Kuulu, kello, kaiu kello	Sound, bell, echo, bell,
Kaiu karjamaan periltä	Echo from the farthest meadows
Kaiu koti kartanohon	Echo even to the home farmyard.
Sä oot suurin lehmistäni	You are the largest of my cattle
Vahvin vasikoistani	The strongest of my calves.
Tuo sä karjani kotihin	Bring ye home the herd
Kalkutellen kartanolle	Clanking to the farmyard,
Saattele iltasavulle	Lead it to the evening smudges
Vielä päivän paistäessa	While yet the sun is shining
Keski illan kellertäissä	In the glow of midevening.
Tuo jonossa Jumalan karja	Bring in a row the cattle of God,
Karja ehtoisan emännän.	The herd of the generous mistress.

Charms for curing or preventing illness are the most often found. Here is one for a bruised or scratched hand: as in the *Kalevala*, a hurt could be cured if one could trace and name its origin.

Hyi! mistä on puuttunut?	Hyi! from what place is distress?
Vaikka vanhoista akkoista?	Is it from an old hag?
Vaikka vattu ranniaista?	Or from the raspberry bushes?
Vaikka seipään sijasta?	Or from the fence post?
Jost'an korppi korvettu	Where the raven turns black
Musta lintu muokatta—Hyi!	The black bird is created—Hyi!

"Hyi" has been translated as "fie," but is not exactly that; it is said explosively and the Finnish pronunciation gives it a whistling sound.

A practical charm to cure hiccough, from Kangasniemi, eastern Finland, was recorded in Winton, Minnesota; it must be said without taking a second breath. It has a good many dialect words, and the alliteration popular in Finnish folk poetry.

Nikko niineen	Hiccough to the heddle [of the loom]
Toinen tuoheen	Second to the bark
Kolmas koivun	Third to the birch
Neljäs neulaan	Fourth to the needle
Viides viittaan	Fifth to the thicket
Kuudes kuuseen	Sixth to the spruce
Seitsemäs seipääseen	Seventh to the pole
Kahdeksas kantoon	Eighth to the stump
Yhdeksäs yllää	Ninth up!
Kymenes kyllää.	Tenth to the neighbor [villager].

From the same source as the above I have another useful charm, for preventing frozen fingers:

Pakkanen puhurin poika,	Cold, son of the wind [lit. "puff"],
Äläkylmää kynsiäin'	Don't chill my finger tips
Älä käsiäin' palele;	Don't freeze my hands;
Palele ves' pajuja,	Freeze the water willows,
Kylmä koivun konkaleita.	Chill the birch chunks.

A Sponge Fishers' Charm

The Greek sponge fishers at Tarpon Springs, Florida, have some very interesting customs and superstitions. For instance, the fishermen will not start out to sea on Tuesday, because they consider it unlucky to start any enterprise on a Tuesday. Neither will they leave port in any new year before Epiphany. When the sponge fishers see the funnel of a cyclone, they carve a cross on the mast of the ship and then stick a knife into it. This saves them from the fury of the storm. The person who performs this charm is committing a sin and must do some form of penance. The fishermen do not hesitate, however, to resort to this charm when in danger.

Ogres: Dracos and Baboulas

Dracos is some wild beast who eats people, as is told in the fairy tale, too; like a monster, one who seizes people and tears them apart and eats them. When we were small we were afraid of him. They would frighten us with the Dracos. He lived on the mountain, and from there he would come. When I was climbing the stairs at home, Dracos would always pull my dress, my legs, with big black nails and fingers; and I would shriek, right after my grandmother told us fairy tales.

They used to frighten us with Baboulas. He was some-thing like the Blackman. Once a mother went down to talk to an acquaintance. And she frightened her child by saying that Baboulas would come and keep her quiet. And she hung up a heavy felt coat upside down. When she returned she found her baby dead of fright.

Omens of Death and Disaster

Tule Lake [the segregation center for Japanese in World War II] was replete with folk beliefs concerning death and ill luck. While we were shown several amulets for good luck such as tiny wooden images to the gods of luck, carved in the Center (1945), and shrine inscriptions and medallions from the old country, the focus was usually upon bad fortune and it was impossible to assemble any-thing like a similar series of good luck omens.

Baishakunin [marriage brokers] held one should not marry a person whose age varied four, seven or ten years from one's own. Seven was, in general, an unlucky num-ber. Northeast was an unlucky direction. Whistling on the part of young people meant evil would befall their house-holds. And if one swept the floor on New Year's Day, or quarreled then, one swept out good fortune for the year or would quarrel the whole year through. A comb, picked up with teeth facing the body, meant bad luck. In these emphases, the temper of the Center was constantly re-vealed. Even more prevalent, however, was reference to death omens.

Typical omens of death included:

If you point at a funeral line, you are next to die.
If three persons are photographed together, the middle one is first to die.
If you feel sorry for a sick animal, you will become ill; if then it dies, you will die.

If a crow cries in a strange, mournful cawing, someone
has died nearby. (Dreams of hawks or snakes, on the
other hand, bring good luck.)

If you cut your nails at night, you will not be at your
parent's deathbed.

Don't sleep with head pointing north—the Buddhist burial
position—or death will follow.

If you kill a spider in the morning, you will kill the spirit
of one who has entered its body while sleeping.

If a cat jumps over a corpse laid out, it will make a vam-
pire of it. (Consequently, said Issei, swords were once
placed beside the dead to prevent this. Nisei were un-
aware of this notion.)

A three-colored cat or black cat can bring good luck, but
most cats do not.

Dreams

If a person dreams that a tooth is pulled without starting blood, it means that some member of his family is going to die. If it is a back tooth, the person will be an aged
one; if a middle tooth, the person will be of medium age;
if a front tooth, the person will be young.

If a person dreams that he is eating white grapes, it
means that it will surely rain the next day.

To dream that a certain man, attired in his finest clothes,
is in a company where the others are not so attired, means
that the man is going to die.

To dream of blood, means that nothing will happen.

If a person dreams that he sees his deceased father or
mother talking angrily to him, it means that he or she
wishes him to pray or make some atonement for him, or
her.

If a person dreams that a large sore breaks and the matter is discharged, it means that he will be able to settle up
all his debts.

If a married man dreams that he is being married, and sees himself attired in his wedding garments, it means that he is going to die.

A man (A) has a certain number of troubles to pass through. If another man (B) dreams that he (A) is dead, he (A) has already passed the first trouble. If a second man (C) dreams that he (A) is dead, he (A) has passed the second trouble. This continues till all are passed.

To dream that the leaves fall to the ground yellow means that there will be an epidemic in the town.

If a person dreams that he sees a naked figure dancing in the air, it means that death will come and release a soul from its body.

If a person dreams that he sees a line of camels traveling single file, it means that angels from heaven are descending to inspire the little children.

If a person dreams of a river, it means that something stands between him and his wishes.

If a person dreams of a woman, it means that he will have happiness. If, however, her hair is disheveled, it means that some member of his family will die soon.

To dream of seeing a cloud in the shape of a camel means there will be no rain and consequently a poor harvest.

To dream of snakes brings bad luck.

To dream of a leafless tree means it will rain the next day.

If a person dreams of an old woman carrying a baby in her arms, it means that some man of the town will die. [The reason being, according to my informant, that the earth is looked upon as the mother of mankind, who carries her children in her bosom when they are dead.]

If a person dreams that there are many priests in his house, he may be sure that on that same day a year hence some member of his household will die. [In Lebanon when a man dies it is the custom for thirty or more priests to attend the funeral ceremony. My informant tells me that the number of priests in each town in Syria is very large in proportion to the population. In B'shory, a town of about seven thousand inhabitants, there are some forty priests.]

If a person dreams of eating human flesh, his life will be short, and his children will perish from the face of the earth.

Water Sleeps

Water sleeps sometime. It makes no noise, is quiet at places, noisy in the day. If a horse drank sleeping water he would die. That's why a horse always blows before drinking at night, to wake the water.

Brujas in Texas

Maria Antonia was emphatic in her expression of belief that there were lots of *brujas* (witches) around, who took delight in doing harm to you personally, or in spreading sickness among your cattle, blighting your crops, or ruining your fruit trees. . . .

There are not only witches in the world, but a class of people whom she styles *gente de chusma,* who seem to be allied to our fairies. They fly about from place to place on the winds. They have sold their souls to the Devil and must never think of God when they die. Their souls fly about from place to place. They will not enter a house where there is mustard. You must take mustard—that in a bottle will do—and make with it a cross upon the wall, alongside of the bed upon which you are to sleep.

Once there was a man down here (Rio Grande City, Texas), who owed a washerwoman five dollars and refused to pay her. Now this washerwoman was a witch, and she filled this man full of worms, but Maria Antonia was called in just in time and gave him a strong emetic and a strong purge, and then dosed him with a decoction of Yerba de Cancer, Yerba Gonzalez, and Guayuli, and expelled thirteen worms (*gusanos*) with green heads and white bodies.

To keep away witches: smoke, drink, or chew powdered *mariguan* every morning. This herb is also given secretly in the food of admirers who have grown insensible to the charms of cast-off and despairing sweethearts.

To cure a man who has been rendered impotent by witchcraft: take out from the lamp hanging in front of the Blessed Sacrament a few drops of oil, put upon a clean rag, and anoint the genitalia. Drop a little more of the oil upon a pan of live coals, saying: "I do this in the name of the Father, Son, and Holy Ghost." Then seek the woman who is beloved, and all obstacles will disappear, but the witch who has caused all the trouble will die at once.

There is another method of using oil, not for divination or warring on witches, but to bewitch, that is, to fascinate men. It consists in stealing from a church some of the oil of baptism, if you can get it; if not, that which is blessed and put into the lamps before the Virgin and saints will do quite as well. And if a girl anoints her lips with it, the man who kisses her

> Will be seized with a strange, wild love;
> He'll heed not the dark world beneath him,
> He'll heed not the heavens above.

To cure a man who has fallen violently in love, through witchcraft: take a shilling's worth of sweet oil, and another of brandy made in Parras (State of Coahuila); mix, and give in doses of a large spoonful until the patient has vomited freely; then give him some beef tea, made hot, but without salt, fat, or tallow. The patient will break out into a profuse sweat, and will vomit again—but he must now be careful of himself, lest he take cold. Let him now eat what he pleases, and go to sleep. When he wakes up in the morning, he will be completely cured of his infatuation.

To keep witches away from you at night: when about to retire, kneel down and say the following prayer, in a low voice:

> *Cuatro esquinas tiene mi casa.*
> *Cuatro angeles que la adoran,*
> *Lucas, Marcos, Juan, y Mateo.*
> *Ni brujas, ni hechiceras.*
> *Ni hombre malhechor.*
>
> *En el Nombre del Padre.*
> *Y del Hijo, y del Espiritu Santo.*
>
> My house has four corners.
> Four angels adore it,
> Luke, Mark, John, and Matthew.
> Neither witches, nor charmers,
> Nor evil-doing man [can harm me].
>
> In the Name of the Father,
> And of the Son, and of the Holy Ghost.

Recite the above three times, and witches can neither harm you nor enter your house.

Witches Outwitted

When Grandmother Eiler was young she had a cow of her own raising, of which she was very proud. One evening at milking time, a certain woman passed through the barnyard, stopped, and looked the cow all over. "I was foolish enough to tell her all about the cow, how gentle she was, how much milk she was giving, and all that, and she said I certainly had a fine cow. Well, the next morning that cow couldn't stand on her feet, and there she lay in the stable till father came home from the mountain, where he was cutting wood. He said it was all plain enough, when I told him everything, but he wondered I hadn't had better sense. However, he knew just what to do. He rubbed the cow all over with asafetida, saying words all the time. And the next day, when I went into the barn, there she stood on her four legs, eating like a hound. Witches can't stand asafetida."

It was this witchwoman who, going to a neighbor's one day on an errand, prolonged her stay without apparent reason, till it was almost night. Though she was very uneasy all the time, and kept saying there was sickness at home and she ought to be there, still she didn't go. Finally, it was discovered that the broom had fallen across the door. When it was taken away, she fairly flew. Of course, this looked very suspicious. But, not to be rash in their judgment, the people of the house sought further proof. So, the next time she came, *salt* was *thrown* under her chair, and there she sat, as though bound until it was removed. Then, as her visits were now considered undesirable, *nails* were driven in her tracks, but the place in the ground marked, in case the footprints became obliterated. It was soon known that she was laid up with sore feet, which refused to heal until the nails were dug up.

Miss K.'s father, when a youth in Germany, had a friend whose rest was disturbed by nightmares. At last he concluded that a witch was troubling him, and proceeded to entrap her by stopping up every crevice and keyhole in the room. (Mindful of the fact, of course, that "for witches this is law—where they have entered in, there also they withdraw.") The next morning he found a beautiful girl cowering in the cupboard. He put her to work as a servant about the house. But eventually, thinking her reformation complete, he married her and lived happily for several years. Sometimes, though, she would sigh, and say she longed to see beautiful France again. One day she was missing, and her little child, just tall enough to reach the keyhole, told how she had removed the stopping for her. She was never seen again, having of course "taken French leave" through the keyhole. The same story is told of a miller in Frederick County. He, too, domesticated a witch-maiden, having caught her in the same way. But, years after, he incautiously opened the keyhole, and found himself a grass widower.

Will-o'-the-wisp

The Negroes are also very much afraid of the will-o'-the-wisp, or *ignis fatuus*. They believe that on a dark night it leads its victim, who is obliged to follow, either in the river, where he is drowned, or in bushes of thorns, which tear him to pieces, the jack-o'-lantern exclaiming all the time, *"Aïe, aïe, mo gagnin toi"*—"Aïe, aïe, I have you."

The old Negro who was speaking to me of the *ignis fatuus* told me that he was born with a caul, and that he saw ghosts on All Saints' Day. He also added he often saw a woman without a head, and he had the gift of prophecy.

Sign of a Hard Winter

In the course of a conversation with an old Welsh coal miner late in the fall, he remarked that we had a long, hard winter before us, and that he was therefore sure of steady work at good wages until spring.

Struck by the absolute confidence of his tone, I inquired how he knew.

"Why," he replied, "look around you. See those weeds. Did you ever see taller? It is the same everywhere—in the fields, in gardens, along the roadside—the weeds are higher than I ever remember seeing them before. That means that we will have the deepest snows the coming winter seen here for many years. The reason is this. The little snowbirds live on the seeds of weeds all winter. If the snow covered up the weeds the birds would starve; so the weeds always grow somewhat higher than the deepest snow will be. When the winter is to be soft and open, with little snow, the weeds only grow a few inches tall. I am an old man and I have never known this sign to fail."

It is pleasant to note that that winter, at least, the old coal miner's faith was justified. Since then I have proved that the same belief is prevalent among the Welsh in all sections of the country. I have even heard it referred to in the pulpit by Welsh clergymen as an instance of God's watchful care over his creatures.

Signs and Countersigns

If you trim your nails on Sunday, you will be sick before the next Sunday.

If you kill a screech owl, some of your kinsfolks will die in twelve months.

If you kill a frog, Massa cow will die.

If your plow trace come unhitched at night while you are turning your mule at the end to take out, you will never live to hitch it again.

If you sweep trash out the door at night, it is a sign Massa gwine to sell you.

If you sneeze on Sunday, the Devil will have you all the week.

If your left eye jump, you are going to laugh.

If your right eye jump, you are going to cry.

The first dove you hear mourn in the new year, if you are going up the hill, you will have good luck all the year;

if you are going down the hill, you will have bad luck all the year.

If you have started anywhere and turn back to avoid bad luck, make a cross-mark on the ground and pull a stran' of hair out of your head and throw it the way you was going.

If you bring an axe or hoe or spade in the house on your shoulder, some of the family will die soon.

If you sneeze at table, it is a sign of death in the family.

If a coal of fire pop and fall in your lap, take it up and hold it in your right pocket till it goes out, you will be sure to get some money soon.

If you are going anywhere and a rabbit crosses you, to avoid bad luck make a cross-mark and take three steps backwards and turn around to your right and spit on the ground.

If you see a whirlwind come towards your house, it is a sign of trouble.

If the whirlwind goes towards the branch or any water, it is a sign of rain.

Halloween Projects

> I wind, I wind, my true love to find,
> The color of his hair, the clothes he will wear,
> The day he is married to me.

Throw a ball of yarn into barn, old house, or cellar, and wind, repeating the above lines, and the true love will appear, and wind with you. To be tried at twelve o'clock at night, October 31.

An old lady of eighty told me that in her youth this was tested by a girl. Some one knowing she was going to make the test hid himself in the barn, and when the proper time came called out, "Timothy B."—the name of a man very much disliked by the girl, who was in love with her. She, thinking he had really appeared, and believing from the sign or project that she would have to marry him, became very ill, and only began to recover when they assured her he was not really there.

Cut up two alphabets, put them face down in water at night; then those that are turned over in the morning are the initials of the one you will marry. [Also, to be tried at midnight] October 31.

Cross-marks

When a Negro is going from you, and you call him, making it necessary for him to retrace his steps, he will make a cross-mark × in the path and spit on it for good luck.

If you meet a stranger in the road, you must turn round, make a cross-mark, and slightly change your direction, for good luck.

When a rabbit runs across the road in front of you, it is a bad sign; cross yourself, or make a × in the road and spit in it, and walk backward over the place where the rabbit crossed. If a rabbit runs across the road behind you, it is a good sign; you have passed the trouble.

If any one wishes to trouble another, he makes a × mark on the path usually traveled by his enemy; the only way to break the spell is to walk round it the first time, afterwards you can walk over.

To stop paths across a field, make cross-marks in it. Negroes may step around the × marks, but they won't step over them.

If the right shoestring becomes accidentally untied, it is a sign that a woman is talking good about you; if the left shoestring, that a woman is talking evil. To prevent the evil, make a cross-mark, put your foot on the mark, and retie the string.

Negroes keep other Negroes from getting over a rail fence by sprinkling powder or graveyard dirt on the rail.

A Cross-mark to Relieve Distress

One Negro woman suffered with a pain in her side, which she firmly believed to be the work of a witch. To exorcise the pain, when it grew severe, she went out into the yard, got on her knees in the sand, and making the following figure of as large dimensions as she could without moving, muttered words to herself that I could never find intelligible, indeed, barely audible, and she would never enlighten me when I asked what she said. Below is the figure she made, very slowly, with her eyes "set," and an intense expression on her face. When she had made a certain number of lines the pain ceased, she said. It appeared that the same number was not always requisite.

Aches and Pains

To wear one earring on the ear next a weak eye will give good eyesight.

An iron ring about the wrist will give strength.

A leather string tied about the wrist cures rheumatism.

A flannel rag round the wrist will cure pain in the arm.

To cure "biles," walk along and pick up the first little white flint rock you see, as it is found sticking in the ground. Rub the boil with the flint, then stick the flint in the ground again, in the same position as you found it. Turn around and leave it, walking backward for a few steps.

To cure chills and fever: after you have had three or four chills, take a piece of cotton string, tie as many knots in the string as you have had chills, go into the woods and tie the string around a persimmon bush, then turn around and walk away, not looking backward.

To wash your face in water in which eggs have been boiled will bring warts.

To take off a wart, take a grain of corn, eat out the heart or white kernel, strike or cut the wart till it bleeds, then take a drop of the blood, put it in the corn where the heart was taken out, and throw the grain to a chicken. The wart will go away.

To strengthen your wind in running, eat half-done corn bread.

Negroes believe that if one borrows a hat from a diseased person, and the wearer sweats round the forehead where the hat rests, he will take the disease.

Don't step over a child; it will stop the child from growing. Stepping over a grown person is a sign of death.

If you cut a mole on your body till it bleeds, it will turn into a cancer and kill you.

To eat a peach, apple, or plum that a bird has pecked is said to be poisonous.

To scratch the flesh with the fingernails till it bleeds is said to be poisonous.

The bite of a "blue-gummed negro" is said to be poisonous.

If a pregnant woman raises her hands high above her head, as for instance to carry a water bucket on the head, it will cause the navel-string of the child to tie about the neck and choke it to death. The child will be born dead. All children so born are supposed to have met their death in this way.

Warts

Put bread soda on a wart to drive it away.

To cure warts cut a notch on a fig tree for every wart you have. Tell no one about it and the warts will go away.

If there is a wart on your hand take an onion and cut it in half; throw one half away, but rub the other on the wart and then bury it. When the onion rots the wart will disappear.

To cure a wart on a horse lead him up to a pecan tree, touch the wart with a nail, and scratch a cross on the tree with the nail. As soon as the cross grows up the wart disappears.

To cure a wart, steal a piece of meat, rub it on the wart, and bury it where the rain dripping from the house will fall on it. When it rots the wart will disappear.

To cure a wart steal a piece of meat, rub it on the wart, and bury it.

To cure warts take as many grains of corn as you have warts, stand on a bayou bridge, and throw them over the left shoulder.

To cure warts tie as many knots in a string as you have warts and bury it in a damp spot under a bridge.

To cure a wart, steal a piece of meat, rub it on the wart, and throw it where a dog will find and eat it.

A way to get rid of a wart is to tie a silk thread around it and stick a hot needle into it.

If anyone has a wart and wishes to get rid of it let him take a piece of meat, rub it on the wart, and wrap it up in a piece of paper. Then he must throw it away without looking at it, and the person who finds it will "catch the wart."

If you have warts fill your mouth with corn, dig a hole in the ground and bury the corn. Soon your warts will disappear.

To cure a wart steal a dishrag, rub it on the wart, and bury it on a bright moonlight night.

Rub warts with the milk from fig trees to make them disappear.

Touch a wart and make a cross on a tree and the wart will disappear.

Say your prayers over a wart and it will disappear.

Say your prayers backward over a wart and it will disappear.

Count warts and they will disappear.

Count a bud on a neighbor's peach tree for each wart you have, and leave without telling the neighbor goodbye, and the warts will disappear.

To cure warts go to the graveyard and "holler" three times like a cat.

Sell a wart and it will disappear.

To cure a tallow bump or other growth: if the moon is decreasing say,

"The moon increases, it decreases" (3 times)
"The moon decreases, it increases" (3 times)
"The moon increases, it decreases" (3 times)

Each time you say one of these you must make the sign of the cross on the growth. If the moon is increasing you must begin this, "The moon decreases," etc. Be sure to begin with the condition opposite that of the moon.

Good Luck and Bad Luck

It is good luck for a squirrel to cross one's path.

It is good luck to see a red bird fly up.

It is good luck to spill wine on the tablecloth.

It is good luck to dream of silver money.

Wednesday is the luckiest day in the week for a wedding.

It is good luck to get white flowers on your birthday.

If one eats peas on New Year's Day, he will have good luck all the year.

A cricket on the hearth will bring good luck.

It is good luck to look at the new moon over your left shoulder.

A windy day for a wedding is a sign of good luck.

It is a sign of good luck to find a pin with the point turned toward you.

When starting on a journey, throw a teaspoon of salt over the right shoulder to insure safety.

To catch a falling leaf means that you will have twelve months of continued happiness.

To find a rusty nail is good luck. The nail should not be picked up, but the ends should be reversed so the luck will come your way.

If two or more people go fishing together, they must all cross the fences at the same time if they are to have good luck at catching fish.

It is bad luck to drop a book and not step on it.

It is bad luck to bring a hoe into the house.

It is bad luck to sweep the floor before the sun rises.

It is bad luck to count the stars.

If one dreams about rats fighting, he will have bad luck.

It is bad luck for one to comb his hair after dark.

It is bad luck to rock an empty chair.

It is bad luck to burn apple trees for firewood.

It is bad luck to wash a garment before it is worn.

It is bad luck to burn the cob when popping corn.

It is bad luck to burn salt.

It is bad luck to count graves.

If one sees a red bird and it flies down, he is sure to have bad luck.

It is bad luck to take the ashes out when there is sickness in the family.

It is bad luck to make a new opening in an old house.

It is bad luck to look at the moon through brush.

It is bad luck to meet a left-handed person on Tuesday.

It is bad luck for sweet potatoes to bloom.

It is bad luck to watch a person out of sight.

It is bad luck for a black hen to come into the house.

It is bad luck to milk a cow on the ground.

It is bad luck to sell a crowing hen.

It is bad luck to break a bird egg.

It is bad luck to spin a chair around on one leg.

It is bad luck to dream of eating cabbage.

It is bad luck to see a pin and not pick it up.

It is bad luck to open an umbrella in the house.

It is bad luck to sit on a pair of scissors.

If you find a cat sitting with her tail to the fire, expect bad luck.

Sunning of bed clothes on Friday will bring bad luck.

Sitting on a trunk invites bad luck.

It is unlucky for a girl to be in church when she is asked to marry.

Ill fortune is created by bringing eggs into the house after sunset.

It is bad luck for a sick person to cut his fingernails while sick.

Spit and Sneeze

If your foot is asleep spit on your finger and make a cross on your foot with it and it will soon be all right.

If you see a caterpillar you must spit; you will be disappointed if you don't.

If you see a cross-eyed person spit to avert the bad luck you would have otherwise.

If you want to hold anything firmly spit on your hands before you take it.

Spit on an insect bite to cure it.

When you have lost anything spit in your hand and

strike it with the forefinger of your other hand. The direction in which it flies is the one you must take to find the lost object.

> "Sneeze on Monday, sneeze for danger;
> Sneeze on Tuesday, kiss a stranger;
> Sneeze on Wednesday, sneeze for a letter;
> Sneeze on Thursday, something better;
> Sneeze on Friday, sneeze for sorrow;
> Sneeze on Saturday, see your beau tomorrow;
> Sneeze on Sunday, hell all the week."

Sneeze on Saturday, joy for Sunday.

Sneeze on Sunday, work hard Monday.

If you sneeze three times a day you are going to be disappointed.

It is a good sign to sneeze.

If you sneeze once a day you are going to miss something.

If you sneeze twice a day you are going to get a kiss.

If someone sneezes at a table where thirteen people are sitting the oldest or the youngest will die within the year.

If the oldest or youngest person at a table sneezes it is a sure sign of death for one of them.

Sneezing at the table is a sign of company for the next meal.

For anyone to sneeze with his mouth full is a sign of death.

If someone sneezes while something is being said it is a sign that it is the truth.

Pins and Needles

If a pin sticks up in your clothes someone is talking about you.

Repeat the letters of the alphabet and the one which

you are saying when the pin falls out is the initial of the person talking.

If you find a pin, pin it in the left shoulder of your dress and make a wish. The wish will come true when the pin comes out.

If you find a pin pick it up with the point toward you and you will have good luck.

If you have a pin in your dress just about to fall out it is a sign that someone is thinking of you.

If you find a pin with the point toward you pick it up and stick it into your clothes upside down; then you will have good luck.

If you see a crooked pin do not pick it up; you will have bad luck if you do.

If you drop a pin and it sticks into the floor company is coming.

If you drop a needle and it sticks into the floor company is coming.

To wear a needle in your clothes brings bad luck.

If you find a needle you are going to catch a beau.

If you find a needle you are going to have a streak of good luck.

When you find a hairpin hang it on a rusty nail and make a wish. When it falls off the wish will come true.

To find a hairpin is a sign that you will receive a letter.

The dropping of a hairpin from the hair indicates losing a friend.

If you find a hairpin hang it on a nail and you will have good luck.

Beliefs about Marriage

Persons married on a cloudy day will have a cloudy life. Similarly, those married on a sunshiny day will have a happy life.

Happy is the bride the sun shines on.

Whoever catches the bride's bouquet will be the next bride.

Some people will only get married when the moon is growing fuller. Then they will prosper.

Others will only get married when the hands of the clock are moving upward.

Swallow a four-leaved clover, and you will marry the first man you meet.

Others say, put a four-leaved clover in your shoe, and you will marry the first man you meet.

If a bride stumbles as she enters her home, she will have many ups and downs. [On account of this superstition, the husband often carries his bride across the threshold.]

If a bride wishes to be prosperous throughout life, she must wear something old, something new, something blue, and something gold. [Others say "borrowed" and "blue" instead of "blue" and "gold."]

If you don't wear out or dispose of your wedding outfit, you will have bad luck.

It is bad luck to wear black at a wedding.

It is bad luck to be married in black.

If a bride wears some person's garter, that person will marry soon if she wears it after the bride does.

In a wedding or birthday cake, the person getting the penny will have riches, the one getting the ring will be the next bride, and the one receiving a bodkin or a thimble will be an old maid.

When sleeping for the first time in a strange bed, name the four corners of the bed, and the first corner seen in the morning will tell whom you will marry.

If you sit on a table, you will not be married for seven years. [Others say it is a sign you wish to be married.]

Place a wishbone over your door, and you will marry the first man entering and shaking hands.

Significance of wedding days:

> Monday for health,
> Tuesday for wealth,
> Wednesday the best day of all.
> Thursday for losses,
> Friday for crosses,
> Saturday no day at all.

Beliefs about Children

Take a newborn baby upstairs or to a high place to make it high-minded.

A baby should be carried upstairs before downstairs so that it will rise in the world.

Never toss a newborn baby up in the air. If you do, it will cause the baby to be feeble-minded.

The third baby boy will be the wisest member of the family.

Bald-headed babies make the brightest students.

If you take a baby downhill before you take it uphill, it will go down in life.

The stork brings babies to whoever he thinks deserves them.

A child should step on its books to keep from missing its lessons.

If a child sleeps with its textbook under its pillow at night, it will know its lesson the next day.

If a baby has large ears, it will be a free-hearted person, but if it has small ears, it will be stingy.

If a baby is born with its hands open, it will have a generous disposition.

If a baby does not clutch a coin that is put in its hand, it will be a spendthrift.

If a baby keeps its hands tightly clinched, it will be stingy.

Put a baby on a floor with a Bible, a deck of cards, and a silver dollar. If it picks up the Bible first, it will be a preacher; if it picks the cards up first, it will be a gambler; and if it picks up the dollar first, it will be a financier.

Place a coin, a bottle, and a book before a child before it is a year old. If it grasps the bottle first, it will be a drunkard; if it takes the money, it will be a rich man; and if it takes the book, it will be a scholar.

Put feathers on the floor in front of a baby girl. If she picks them up, she will be a good housekeeper, but if she lets them lie unnoticed, she will be a slovenly one.

If you crack the first louse found in a baby's head on the bottom of a tin cup, the baby will be a good singer.

A baby born with a large mouth will be a good singer.

If a child sings in bed, it will wet the bed.

It is bad luck to name a baby for a dead person.

To change a baby's name after you have named it will cause it to have bad luck all of its life.

It is bad luck to put a baby's dress on over its head before it is a year old.

It is bad luck to cut a baby's hair before the baby is a year old.

Always kiss a baby boy, for kisses bring good luck.

It is a sign of good luck for a baby to cry when being christened.

To trim a baby's fingernails before it is a month old will cause it to have fits.

A baby will be a thief if its fingernails are trimmed before it is a year old.

If you bite a baby's fingernails, it will steal when it grows up.

To keep a baby from being sick, bathe it in dirty dishwater.

Wearing a rabbit's foot around a baby's neck will prevent sickness.

Hang a small bag of sulphur around a baby's neck, and it will never be sick.

If a baby is put in the first April shower, it will always be healthy.

If a newborn baby has thick hair, it will be sickly.

Asthma in a child may be cured by placing a lock of its hair in a hole of a post or tree above the child's head.

Let a chicken fly over a child's head to cure chickenpox.

To keep a baby from having colic, blow tobacco smoke on its stomach.

To prevent colic in a baby, pour hot water into a shoe and give it to the baby to drink.

A baby will have the colic if a teakettle boils in a room where the baby is.

If you rock an empty cradle, the baby will have the colic.

If a child has the croup, cut off a bunch of its hair and bury it on the east side of a creek for instant cure.

To cure a very young baby of croup, tie a black silk cord around its neck.

To cure earache, give the child marrow from the bone of a hog.

Nutmeg tied around a baby's neck will cure hives.

If a child steps on a rusty nail and hurts its foot, put goose grease on the nail and drive it in the east side of a sycamore tree to prevent infection.

A child will not have influenza if it wears sulphur in its shoes.

Hoodoo

Write the name of an enemy eleven times on a piece of paper. Place a lighted candle on it; when the candle burns down and the paper begins to burn his trouble begins.

A person who is hoodooed usually has some peculiar mark appear on his body.

If a hoodoo bag is thrown into running water the bad luck falls on the person placing the bag.

If a person who has been hoodooed crosses running water the hoodoo loses its effect.

A hoodoo bag contains certain weeds, brick, dirt, red flannel, etc. It is most effective when the weeds, brick, and dirt come from a grave.

Some evidences of hoodoo are: cards stacked over the door, nails stacked on a window, and a bag on the tester of a bed.

If a horse is hoodooed, place his foot on the ground, then cut the grass in the space so covered, and when the grass grows level again the horse will be all right.

To become a hoodoo you must sell your soul to the Devil. To do this on the darkest night of the month go out alone into a field and wait for him to appear. He will do this exactly at midnight in the form of a black bird or shadow. After you have made your agreement with him he is your master, but he will help you to accomplish anything within his power.

A snake bone in the pillow is a sign of hoodoo.

A hoodoo is sometimes prepared of feathers, snake bone, and horsehair.

Black pepper and salt sprinkled on the steps are a sign of hoodoo.

Knots in a feather pillow are a sign of hoodoo.

Do not burn red candles, for it is a sign of hoodoo. (You may be hoodooed by doing so.)

Sometimes people visiting sick persons make "bad mouth"—that is, they say that they wish the sick person to recover, etc., but they are really there to do him evil. If you wish to test a visitor: just after he has left, melt some lead and then let it cool. If it is smooth when cool his visit was all right, but if it is rough he was there with evil purpose.

Wear a silver coin around the ankle to prevent hoodoo.

Warnings of hoodoo may come in three messages: first warning—; second, a loaf of bread covered with pitch on the doorstep; and third, a tiny coffin left on the doorstep. After the third the victim will die.

You may be hoodooed through your teeth. Have them pulled to break the hoodoo.

If a person's illness can be cured in no other way he is hoodooed.

Do not sleep on a feather pillow or mattress, for a common means of hoodoo is through feathers.

The harness fell off of a horse every time an old woman drove over a ditch in front of an old witch's place. The old witch had some kind of hoodoo on the spot.

If you sleep on a bed which has feather wreaths in it you will be hoodooed. The wreaths are placed there by someone wishing to hoodoo you.

When a horse's mane, tail, or forelock are full of queer little knots it is a sign that the witches have been riding him the night before.

You can "conjer" a horse—that is, make him obedient to your will—if you carry an ear of corn under your arm and then feed it to him.

If a woman is hoodooed and made physically weak as a result of it, let her take three pieces of hoop iron, place them in a pitcher, and draw water over them. Then she must drink this water, which will counteract the effect of the hoodoo.

An old crippled Negro, who had a lump in her leg, claimed that it was a frog put there by a hoodoo. She died as a result of the trouble.

Negroes' wrists "open." They "close" them by tying little pieces of red flannel around them. (They sometimes "open" when they are doing even such light work as washing dishes.)

A Negro cook will sometimes put a rusty nail in the bail of a pot to keep the contents from boiling over. She hoodooes it.

Fold back the thumb to prevent the effects of the evil eye.

If you will take the main feather from a black rooster's tail, hold it in your hand, and draw it through your sweetheart's hand she will accept your suit.

Flyting with Witches

While living in one of their various log cabin residences along the Pennsylvania-West Virginia border, the Bayles family discovered that certain hardships which they were experiencing were due to the witchcraft of a neighbor. She troubled them at first by causing their rest to be disturbed by a number of cats, who would suddenly appear in the room, frolic over the beds, and then disappear just as mysteriously as they had come, since the house was shut up for the night and there was no opening through which animals of their size could enter or leave. Following this, the Bayleses were visited by a sudden shaking of the whole house, which was repeated night after night, sometimes throwing them out of their beds. To his wife's questions about these doings, Bayles would make no reply except that "the Devil was about; but he knew who was doing it; he'd fix them." His opportunity apparently came when the witch paid them a visit, during which Bayles kept a close watch on her, and finally thought he had detected her in an effort to burn the house down by inserting a live coal between the log wall and the inner board wall of the cabin. He immediately accused her. She, of course, appeared shocked by the charge, but he persisted in it; told her that he knew of her evil doings: that she had come at first "with cats," then "with trying to shake the house down"; and finally, heaping invectives on her, he ordered her to go and never return. She fled hastily, and they neither saw her nor were troubled by her magic again.

At one time Bayles was called to Bellaire, Ohio (about forty miles away from where he was then living), to help a girl who had fallen into a witch's power and was wasting away, no local practitioner being able to free her from the enchantment. Upon arriving at the victim's home, he straightway set about his spells, and took up his quarters in another house near at hand—apparently in order to practice his magic in greater seclusion. However, he gave the girl certain explicit directions: not to give anything to the witch or to any outsider; not to admit the witch, or any other person outside the family, into the house; and if she saw the witch coming, to close and fasten the doors and windows, and try to find a place in the house where she could not be seen. But if the witch spoke to her, then she should reply by cursing the intruder and ordering her away.

The girl promised to fulfill her instructions, of course; but three times after that she let the sorceress enter the house, and each time excused herself to Bayles by saying that she had been deceived: she had thought the visitor was her sweetheart. On the last of these occasions, Bayles himself met the witch as he was approaching the house and she was leaving it. She stopped and looked steadfastly at him, and he suddenly realized that a strange feeling was coming over him. If he "hadn't thought what he was about," she would have cast a spell over him also. But he stopped in his tracks and "throwed the spell away from off'n him"; whereupon the witch departed, and he went on to the house. This time he told the girl that if she did not follow his orders in every detail, he could do nothing for her—he was wasting his time, and might better go home. This threat frightened her into strict obedience, and the next time her enemy came, every door and window was fastened and the girl was nowhere in sight. Round the house went the witch, trying each door and window; and finally, looking through a small aperture, she spied her victim. Immediately she called to the girl, asking why she was shut out, and if this were the way to treat a friend.

The girl answered that the witch was no friend of hers, but had done her much harm, and would do more if she could. Then, cursing her enemy, the girl commanded her to depart. When the witch heard this, she took to flight, screaming "so that you could have heard her a mile away," and shortly afterward died.

Mrs. Rogers, who believes as firmly as Mrs. Sayre in the efficacy of flyting, told me this anecdote: As she was going by the house of an old woman who was reputed a witch (and whose dwelling she never passed without muttering a few precautionary curses), the woman suddenly ran out of doors and came straight toward her, crying "Chicken guts, chicken feathers, chicken guts, chicken feathers!" This scared Mrs. Rogers so badly that she fled at full speed, screaming out oaths and invectives as she ran. She attributed her safety then and afterward to the curses she had leveled at the old woman; for she was sure that the above words carried a malign spell.

To Foil a Witch

If a witch should bewitch you, she will probably appear to you next time as an animal. Shoot the animal with a silver bullet if you desire to injure the witch.

Lumbermen wrap themselves in fresh deerskin to keep off witches.

Any witch or ghost may be destroyed by merely asking them what they want of you.

To frighten witches away, sprinkle salt around the house.

Your milk will be hard to churn if witches are in it. To get rid of them set the churn in a chimney corner and whip the milk with a switch or drop a dime in the churn.

Plants, Birds, Animals and Insects

It is bad luck if fruit trees bloom twice a year.

A four-leaf clover is good luck, but a five-leaf is bad.

Plants will not grow if you thank the giver.

Steal flower cuttings and they will grow.

Tear flower petals from the flower and say, "He loves me; he loves me not," to find out his feelings toward you.

Put bits of tobacco on fern pots to make ferns grow.

A person who raises plants easily has a "green thumb."

Plant a cedar in a yard, and by the time it is large enough to shadow a coffin, someone will die.

All root crops will make all tops and no roots if planted in the light of the moon.

Plant potatoes in third quarter of moon in a fruitful sign.

Plant turnip seed the twenty-fifth of July, wet or dry.

Onions will rot if dug in the sign of the heart.

Plant corn when the sign is in the head.

Plant cucumbers in June when the sign is in the twins.

Weeping willows bring bad luck.

Plant potato eyes with the eyes up so that they may see.

Plant sweet peas after dark to insure blooming.

Plant potatoes in the dark of the moon so that you will have plenty of potatoes and few vines.

Plant plants that grow above ground, as lettuce, in the light of the moon.

Plant flower seeds in the "flower woman" in the light of the moon.

Make a wish when two birds are seen approaching together.

A screeching owl means bad luck.

Take off your right shoe and turn it upside down to drive away a screech owl.

Owls hooting in daytime foretell death.

A bird flying against a house means bad luck.

Redbirds bring good luck.

Make a wish when you see a redbird. The wish will come true if the bird flies up or toward the east.

Your wish will come true if you throw three kisses to the first robin you see in the spring.

If a bat flies low enough to touch your head, you will die.

You will see someone unexpectedly if you see a redbird.

Put salt on a bird's tail for luck.

When you hear the first dove of the spring, step back three steps and you will find a hair the color of your future mate's.

Your business will prosper if you see three birds fly in single file.

There will be sorrow if you see one buzzard in the air.

Crows bring bad luck.

Low flying swallows mean rain.

Birds singing in a rain mean the rain will stop.

It is a sign of death when a bird peeks in a window.

The first bluebird you see in the spring brings luck.

If you see three birds sitting on a wire, make a wish before they move away.

If a black cat crosses the path in front of you, turn back home for luck.

It is good luck for a light colored cat to cross your path.

Don't move a cat when you move.

If a black cat comes to your home to stay, it is good luck.

If cats yowl much at night it means death.

A white mule is bad luck.

When a horse rolls over in the dirt, the number of times it rolls over is the number of one hundred dollar bills it is worth.

Howling dogs mean a death.

Don't kill a woolly worm crossing your path.

It is good luck for a spider to spin its web down in front of you.

It is bad luck to kill a spider.

If you handle toads, you will have warts.

If you kill a toad, a cow will give bloody milk.

Don't milk a cow on the ground; she will go dry.

Beat an old pan when bees swarm, and they will settle.

Set an odd number of eggs under a hen.

Put iron pieces around a setting goose so that thunder will not kill young goslings in the shell.

A snake will swallow its young if danger approaches.

When you kill a snake, it will not die until sunset.

Cut off a snake's tail and it will grow back together.

Meat shrinks if hogs are killed when the moon is decreasing.

Kill hogs when the moon is increasing to have more meat.

A cat will suck a child's breath if they sleep together.

Kill a snake, kill an enemy.

Wearing peacock feathers is bad luck.

Don't kill flies at the end of the year; every fly killed means a hundred dollar loss.

When you see a white horse, wish; the wish will come true.

Carry a rabbit's foot for luck.

The left hind foot of a rabbit killed in a cemetery is lucky.

Carry a rabbit's foot in your hip pocket to ward off evil.

To keep your dog home, cut the tip from his tail and put it under the front doorstep; he will not leave.

If sharks follow ships, there will be a death.

Don't kill a frog.

It is bad luck to kill a female dog.

It is bad luck to kill a cat.

A cat looking in a mirror means bad luck.

It is good to see stamping white horses.

A snake killed at sunrise will never die.

When a cat lies on its back there will be a storm.

When a dog lies on its back the weather will change.

It will rain when dogs eat grass.

Company will come when a cat washes its face.

It will turn cold when a cat lies with its back to the fire.

Nudity and Planting Customs

In the spring of 1920, when I lived in southwest Missouri, a fisherman from Joplin was walking through the woods just at dawn. He saw a man and a woman in a little field. "They was both stark naked," he said, "chasing each other up and down like rabbits." The clearing he indicated was near my home, and I knew the couple who lived there. They were quiet, hardworking folk. The man came from a good backwoods family, and the woman attended the village church. Such people might "cut up" a little at some drunken party, but I couldn't imagine them running naked out of doors at four o'clock in the morning. I did not believe the fisherman's tale. Several days later I mentioned it to a friend who had lived in the neighborhood all his life. "Yes, I've heard of such doings," he said with a grin. "It's supposed to make the corn grow tall." When I asked where people ever got such a notion, he said that doubtless the pioneers brought it from Tennessee, or Kentucky, or Virginia. "It's just a kind of a joke," he added, "because nobody really believes in them things nowadays. But I'll bet that young fellow's grandpappy thought it was just as true as God's own gospel."

Since that time I have become intimately acquainted with the people who live in the Ozark country, and interviewed hundreds of old-timers. There is no doubt in my mind that many early settlers believed that newly cleared fields were benefited by some kind of nude skylarking. Many of them thought that certain crops grew better if the persons who sowed the seed were naked. This sort of thing is not widely practiced today, and most of my neighbors say that they never even heard of it. But I know that such tilling and planting rites were carried out, in isolated places, less than thirty years ago.

There are several tales about a "wild clan" in southwest Missouri who produced phenomenal turnips by reason of some secret magic. A very old woman said that before sunrise on July 25, four grown girls and one boy did the planting. "They all stripped off naked," she told me. "The boy started in the middle of the patch with them four big gals a-prancin' round him. It seems like the boy throwed all the seed, and the gal kept a-hollering 'Pecker deep! Pecker deep!' And when they got done, the whole bunch would roll in the dust like some kind of wild animals. There ain't no sense to it," the old woman added, "but them folks always raised the best turnips on the creek."

Once in McDonald County, Missouri, a giggling farm girl led me to the top of a high ridge. "I'll show you something funny," she promised. Down in the holler was a clearing with a tiny cabin. After awhile we saw a man and two nude women romping and tumbling on the ground, in a freshly-plowed garden patch. "Them people belong to the New Ground church, and that's their religion," the girl told me. "They've got beds in the house, but they think it's better to waller in the dirt." She said nothing about crops or planting. But the earth in that particular spot was prepared for seeding, and later in the season I saw turnips growing there.

An old gentleman in Aurora, Missouri, told me that the early settlers had a ritual for sowing flax. Just before sunup the farmer and his wife appeared in the field, both naked. The woman walked ahead of the man, and the man did the sowing. They chanted or sang a rhyme with the line "Up to my ass, an' higher too!" Every few steps the man threw some of the seed against the woman's buttocks. Up and down the field they went, singing and scattering seed, until the planting was done. "Then," as my informant put it, "they just laid down on the ground and had a good time." It was considered essential that no outsider should see the sowing or hear the song, because if that were to happen the crop would be a failure.

A farmer near the Missouri-Oklahoma line was telling about the superstitions of some "peckerwood folks" who lived there in the early 1890s. "Soon as they got their bread planted, that fellow would take his wife out to the patch at midnight. He'd make her take off every stitch of clothes, and run around the crop three times. And then he would throw her right down in the dirt, and have at it till she squealed like a pig!" This procedure was said to protect the corn against damage from frost, drought, crows, and cutworms. One of the girls in this family had married a Cherokee, and my informant regarded the practice as part of an Indian ceremony. But several old Cherokees whom I interviewed said that they never heard of any such foolishness.

Most farmers believe that cucumbers should be planted "when the sign's in the arms," which means that the moon is in Gemini. But many old-timers think that the main thing is to get the seed covered before daylight on May 1, by a naked man in the prime of life. It is believed that the quality of a cucumber depends upon the virility of the planter. Cucumbers grown by women, children, or old men never amount to much. There are several vulgar jokes and stories about this. To say that a girl "ought to be raising cucumbers" means that she needs a vigorous young husband.

PROVERBS

In his definitive study of the proverb, Archer Taylor states that "no definition will enable us to identify positively a sentence as proverbial. Those who do not speak a language can never recognize all its proverbs." Someone has called proverbs "the wit of one and the wisdom of many," and Leonato's line in *Much Ado About Nothing*, "patch grief with proverbs," reminds us why they are needed. But to distinguish the proverb from the literary aphorism, the popular comparison, the Wellerism, the slogan, and the conventional phrase is an extremely difficult task.

Basically metaphoric, proverbs involve the perception of general truths, basic associations, and awareness of likeness and difference. They have long literary as well as long folk traditions and have an amazing ability to remain constant in form over great periods of time. Some scholars have seen them as a manifestation of an essential stage in the evolution of man's thought. Edwin Loeb, for example, has suggested that proverbs are used only by people of property (cattle-raisers as opposed to migrant hunters) and that the form indicates a movement of thought from the stage of sympathetic magic toward deductive and inductive reasoning. Among primitive groups they may serve as the major ethical, educational, and legal guides, and even in a highly industrial nation they have a great deal to do with the maintenance of group attitudes.

Any study of the proverb must begin with Taylor's *The Proverb* (Hatboro, Pa., 1962) quoted above. One can use his bibliography to find further, more specialized readings.

Yiddish Proverbs

GOD AND FATE

Gott fiert die ganze welt.
God governs the whole world [All's right with the world].

Gott weist dem emess.
God knows the truth [said by a person who is unjustly accused].

Gott is a dayin emess.
God is a just judge.

Gott vet helfen.
The Lord will provide [help].

Es is baschert.
It is fated [foreordained].

Alles is baschert.
Everything is predestined.

Der mensch tracht, un Gott lacht.
Man thinks, and God laughs [Man proposes and God disposes].

Gott nemmt mit ein hand, un git mit der andere.
God takes with one hand, and gives with the other.

Gott stroft mit ein hand, un benscht mit der andere.
God punishes with one hand, and blesses with the other.

Gott schickt die refue far der make.
God sends the remedy before the disease.

Wemen Gott will erquicken, kennen menschen nit dersticken.
Whom God wishes to succor, men cannot destroy.

Az Gott will geben, git er breit mit putter; un az er will nit, git er kein breit eich nit.

When God wishes to give, he gives bread and butter;
when he does not wish to, he does not give even bread.

Af morgen zoll Gott zorgen.
Let God care for the morrow.

Dem rosche geht af der welt, dem tzadek af jener welt.
The wicked fare well in this world; the saints, in the life
to come.

WISDOM AND FOLLY

Wu teire, dort is chochmo.
Where there is a knowledge of the Scriptures, there is
wisdom.

Die teire hot kein grund nit.
The Scriptures have no bottom [require endless study].

Teire is die beste s'cheire.
A knowledge of the Scriptures is the best wares.

Wu me darf meach, helft nit kein keach.
Where you need intellect, physical strength will not do.

A mamzer zu zein, abie klug zu zein.
It's worth being an illegitimate child, if one can be bright
therewith [this refers to the superstition that all illegitimate children are bright].

Freg nit bam klugen, freg bam genitten.
Do not ask the wise man, ask the experienced one.

Besser fun a gratsch a patsch, eider fun a nar a kusch.
Better a blow from a wise man than a kiss from a fool.

*Besser mit a klugen zu verlieren eider mit a nar zu gewin-
nen (or gefinnen).*
Better to lose with a wise man than to win (or find) with
a fool.

Ein nar ken mehr fregen eider zehn kluge kennen entferen.
One fool can ask more questions than ten wise men can
answer.

Az a nar warft arain a stein in gorten kennen zehn kluge nit aroisnemmen.
When a fool throws a stone into the garden, ten wise men cannot get it out.

Der klugster mensch benart zach.
The wisest man is guilty of folly.

CHARITY

Gutzkeit is besser fun frumkeit ["*klugkeit*" in another version].
Kindness is better than sanctimony ["wisdom" in another version].

Me darf leben un losen leben.
Live and let live.

Schit nit kein salz af die wunden.
Don't throw salt on people's wounds.

S'is schlecht zu essen fremden breit.
It is hard to eat a stranger's bread.

A fremder pelz waremt nit.
A stranger's cloak does not keep one warm.

Fremds iz nit kein eigens.
What you get from another is not like your own.

Me zoll nit darfen onkummen zu laiten.
Pray that you may not have to be dependent on others.

A karger zollt taier.
A niggard pays dear.

Es is a mitzva a chazir a hor arois zu raissen.
It is a virtuous deed to pull a hair out of a pig [stingy person].

Az me will nit geben Yankefen, git men Eisefen.
If you won't give to Jacob, you'll have to give to Esau. [If you are too stingy to give in a good cause, your money will be taken from you by your enemies.]

THE FAMILY

Besser dos kind zoll weinen eider der foter.
Better the child cry than the father.

A schlechte mame is nitto.
There is no such thing as a bad mother.

Kleine kinder, kleine freiden;
Greisse kinder, greisse leiden.
Little children, little joys;
Bigger children, bigger sorrows.

Jeder mutter denkt ihr kind is schein.
Every mother thinks her child is beautiful.

Ein kind iz azei wie ein eig.
Having an only child is like having one eye.

Besser af der welt nit zu leben eider onkummen zu a kind.
It is better not to live than to be dependent on children.

Man un weib zeinen ein leib.
Husband and wife are one flesh.

Wu zwei schlofen af ein kischen,
Darf zach der dritter nit mischen.
Where two sleep on one pillow, a third person has no right
  to interfere [in a family quarrel].

Coplas from New Mexico

El que comparte y reparte
y en repartir tiene tino,
siempre deja, de contino,
para sí la mejor parte.

The one who divides and distributes
and who knows how to have his own **way**,
every time he makes divisions,
can get the best part for himself.

Las tres desdichas del mundo,
que el hombre puede tener,
es vivir en casa ajena,
pedir y haber menester.

The three evils of this world,
that a man can ever suffer,
are to live in another's house,
to beg, and to be a pauper.

Orillas de una laguna
me dió sueño y me dormí.
¡Hablaron de Jesucristo,
y no habián de hablar de mí!

Standing by the lake shore
I was tired and went to sleep.
They gossiped about Christ,
So what couldn't they have said about me!

El verte en poder ajeno
hace delirar mi vida;
pero hay un refrán que dice:
'Dios tarda pero no olvida.'

To see you in another's arms
gives me the fevers and sweats;
but a saying goes that "God
delays but never forgets."

Dices que ya no me quieres,
no me da pena maldita,
que la mancha de la mora
con otra verde se quita.

You say you no longer love me,
I feel no sorrow whatever,
for the stain of the berry
with a green one is removed.

'Vale más algo que nada,'
dice el refrán castellano;
entré á la primer posada,
me tomaron de la mano.

"Anything's better than nothing,"
says the Castilian refrain;
I entered the first inn,
I was taken by the hand.

Unos son los que corren la liebre
y otros llegan allí de rondón.
Los que corren se quedan con fiebre
y los otros alcanzan el don.

Some people chase the rabbit,
and some others come to watch.
The ones that run get the fever,
the others get the benefit.

Cuatro palomitas blancas
sentadas en un romero,
una á la otra se decían,
'No hay amor como el primero.'

Four white doves
perched on a rosemary,
said one to the other,
"There's no love like the first."

¿Para qué es tanto engrimiento
desde la flor al cogollo?
Si al cabo la mejor planta
la riega el más triste arroyo.

Why act with such foolish pride
from the root to the top leaf
if the best plants in the world
are watered by the poorest streams?

Vale más morir á palos
que de celos padecer.
Vale más querer á un perro
que no una ingrata mujer,
que un perro es agradecido
cuando le dan de comer.

Better to die by blows
than from jealousy fade away.
Better to love a dog
than a thankless woman,
for a dog is grateful
when he is fed.

Nadien diga en este mundo,
'De esta agua no beberé,'
por revuelta que la vea
le puede apretar la sé.

Let no one say in this world,
"Of this water I won't drink,"
no matter how muddy it looks
it may quench your thirst.

Dicen que lo negro es triste,
yo digo que no es verdá;
tú tienes los ojos negros
y eres mi felicidad.

They say black is sad,
I say it isn't so;
Your eyes are black
and you are my happiness.

Les diré que con la muerte
no hay humana resistencia,
no hay poder, no hay eselencia,
no hay casa que sea fuerte.

I will tell you that against death
there's no human resistance,
there's no power, there's no excellence,
there's no house which is strong.

Proverbs from Massachusetts

Don't stay till the last dog's hung.
The still pig eats the swill.
No man dies without an heir.
Three removes are as bad as a fire.
What comes over the Devil's back is sure to go under
his belly.
A short horse is soon curried.
Dunghills rise and castles fall.

A Proverbial Rhyme

Them as buys meat, buys bones;
Them as buys land, buys stones;
Them as buys eggs, buys shells;
Them as buys ale, buys nothin' else.

Gullah Proverbs

Take no more on your heels than you can kick off with your toes.

A good run is better than a bad stand.

Everything good to eat is not good to talk.

Every man for hisself and God for we all.

Roll your applecart right on.

Every grin teeth don't mean laugh.

Every shut eye don't mean sleep.

Feed you with the corn and choke you with the cob.

Young folks, listen what old folks say,
When danger is near keep out of the way.

Singing in the morning, hawk will catch you before night.

Still water runs deep.

Geechee Proverbs

Better let well do done.

Live, learn, die, and forget all.

'Tain't no good to kill de crane after he done fly ober de roof er de house and call fer a corpse.

Day's short as ever, time's long as it has been.

Day's des a arm long, you can reach clean across it.

Night's a shadder, day's a shine,
Gone 'fo' you catch it gwine.

Mistakes ain't haystacks, or dar'd be mo' fat ponies den dar is.

Burn up de axe-helve dat can't hold up de blade.

Let the flatiron rust dat puts cats' faces on de cloze.

Don't fly so high dat you lit on a candle.

Trouble follers sin as sho' as fever follers a chill.

Fire don't crack a full pot.

Des hold up your end er do beam, an' de world'll roll on.

De fool'll hang a horseshoe on a dead man's do' for luck.

It rains, and every man feels it some day [this is the same as, "Fortune changes. You may have something to-day, and I tomorrow"].

A hard head makes a soft back [this is equivalent to, "If a child will not be admonished, he will be beaten"].

Stand further better more than beg pardon [this means, "It is much better to keep out of trouble than to beg pardon after getting into it"].

Whickerin' mares don't hatter ax de road to de cabin whar de ol' folks live [the whickering mares are little brown birds known by that name to the plantation-hands. They are said to fly in flocks, and to come out about a cabin only when some old dweller therein approaches death. At such times they fly and whicker anear, and cannot be driven away].

RIDDLES

Riddles represent a very early means of literary expression. They could be one of the forms from which poetry started. In fact, some of the more elaborate riddles, such as those known to the Anglo-Saxons, are almost impossible to distinguish from short lyrics. However, most riddles are naïve, relying on the unexpected or on a simple juxtaposition of contrasting ideas. Such riddles are similar to jokes and frequently provoke laughter. They seldom appeal to a person whose mind has been highly educated or disciplined.

Societies such as ours no longer use the riddle as a means of passing knowledge from one generation to another, although we retain them to tease and puzzle children and to display wit. However, there was a time when riddles served a definite function in rites associated with crucial events such as marriage, war, puberty, and rain making. In folk and primitive societies, success or failure in solving a riddle may serve as means of foretelling the future, of establishing patterns of inclusion or exclusion, of learning the attitude of a deity. Such riddles are frequently obscene, and their presence in the English folk Christmas had much to do with the Puritan opposition to that celebration.

A good beginning toward a study of the riddle can be made through Archer Taylor's *English Riddles from Oral Tradition* (Berkeley, Calif., 1951). The notes and bibliography in this book are especially useful.

Polish Riddles

Why does the crow fly to the woods? (Because the woods can't fly to the crow.)

What kind of trees grow in the woods? (Round trees.)

Under what kind of bushes do rabbits sit when the rain comes? (Under wet bushes.)

Why does the dog wag the tail? (Because the tail can't wag the dog.)

It doesn't eat or drink, but runs and strikes. (A clock.)

Two brothers run away, the other two try to catch them but never can. (Four wheels of a car or wagon.)

What kind of a ghost blows your hat off, but you can't see him? (The wind.)

What grows in the woods and has a body and leaves, then leaves the woods and carries a body and soul? (Cradle or bed.)

Lithuanian Riddles

The bush is full of eyes, but does not see at all. (Potato.)

A lord is black like a Gypsy, and the red kittens whip him. (A pot on fire.)

Around the house are many lakes. (Windows.)

The girl is of clay, her heart is of linen, and her head of fire. (Candle.)

The girl is slender, her plait is thick, and plenty of knits. (Hemp.)

Two rings, two lizards, and they bite everybody whom they can reach. (Scissors.)

The body is of wood, the head is of iron and has only one tooth. (Ax.)

The fish is cold, her head is of iron, and teeth are along the entire belly. (Saw.)

He is going all day and all night, but cannot ever move from his place. (Watch.)

He is blind and dumb, has no tongue, but speaks several languages. (Pen.)

A blind and dumb man sits in an honorable place, and to everybody tells the truth. (Mirror.)

He is without head and without hands, but his body has plenty of ribs. (Ladder.)

The body is of wood, the shoe of iron, and he serves all people, living as well as dead. (Spade.)

One has not caught the animal and not yet tasted it, but licks the fingers already. (A woman before starting to catch fleas.)

On the neck is a beam, on the hands small bells. (Water carrier with two pails.)

From the middle the sows were driven out, but the small pigs were left in the corners. (A lazy girl has swept the room.)

Twelve eagles, more than fifty-two pigeons, more than three hundred wagtails. (Year: months, holy days, and workdays.)

An animal eats on a living table. (To suckle a child.)

Under a blanket someone says: dig, dig, dig. (Water in a frozen river.)

Who makes it, has no need of it; who buys it, has no use for it; and who uses it, can neither see nor feel it. (Coffin.)

When it is nice weather, he sits in a corner; when it is raining, he runs outside. (Umbrella.)

When it is living, it stinks; when it is dead, it smells good. (Pig.)

One went at night and lost his silver buckle; the moon found it, but only the sun caught it. (Dew.)

Syrian Riddles

He cooks his meals on his head for someone who sits near him to eat. (Turkish pipe.)

There are three persons. (a) One is sitting down, and will never get up. (Stove.) (b) The second eats as much as is given to him, and yet is always hungry. (Fire.) (c) The third goes away, and never returns. (Smoke.)

A person looks up at night and sees a kettle full of potatoes, but the next morning when he wakes up he doesn't find any. (Stars.)

There is a man who passes you on the street, but you can't see him. (The wind.)

The Princess of Halef sends to the Princess of Lebanon a horse, which is harnessed in the hind quarters, but its head is free. (A needle.)

A little thing before your eyes all the time. (Eyelash.)

A child, though born tonight, is yet an old man and his white hair fills the whole room. (Light of a lamp.)

Not larger than an eye, and yet it has thousands of eyes. (Thimble.)

He is quite mute, blind, and deaf, yet he has seen and heard all that has occurred in the past, and he will see and hear all that is to come in the future: just now he tells us all. (A book.)

Like the brow of my beloved, or the half of her bracelet, or like a golden cup that is hers, and still a gold coin against a garment of blue velvet. (The new moon.) Not called "riddle" [häzzûrä] by the Syrians, but mōhǎmā, which is almost a riddle, but self-explanatory.

Something alive which, if taken to another land, will die. (A fish.)

Mexican Riddles

Y lo es   And it is
Y no lo es   And it isn't
¿Qué es?   What is it?
    (*Hilo.*)   (Thread.)

Tito, tito   Tito, tito
Con su capotito   With his little cape
Subió al cielo   Climbed to heaven and
Y dió un gritito.   Gave a little shout.
    (*El cohete.*)   (The skyrocket.)

Pennsylvania Dutch Riddles

En eisner Gaul,
Un en fläche Schwäntzel.
Wie de stärker das des Gäuliche springt
We kürtzer das sei Schwäntzel werd.
            (*Nodle un Fadem.*)

An iron horse,
With a flaxen tail.
The faster that the horse does run,
The shorter does his tail become.
           (Needle and thread.)

Wer es macht, der sagt es net,
Wer es nehmt der kent es net,
Wer es kent der will es net.
           (*Falsh Geld.*)

Whoever makes it, tells it not,
And whoever takes it, recognizes it not,
And whoever recognizes it wants it not.
           (Counterfeit money.)

Was geht zu der Deer rei un glemt sich net?
Was geht uf der Ofa un brent sich net?
Was geht uf der Disch un shamt sich net?
                              (*Die Sonn.*)

What goes through the door without pinching itself?
What sits on the stove without burning itself?
What sits on the table and is not ashamed?

                                        (The sun.)

Was is das?
              So hoch ass en Haus,
              So nidder ass en Maus,
              So rauh ass en Riegel,
              So glatt ass en Spiegel,
              So bitter ass Gall,
              Un is gut fer uns all.
                              (*Kescht.*)

              As high as a house,
              As low as a mouse,
              As rough as a rail,
              As smooth as a mirror,
              As bitter as gall,
              But sweet to us all.
                              (Chestnut.)

Was is das?
              Es is en Dierli,
              Es heest Maureli,
              Es hot nein Häut,
              Un beist alle Leut.
                  (*En Zweivel.*)

              There is a little animal,
              Its name is Maureli,
              It has nine skins,
              And bites everybody.
                              (An onion.)

Was fern Vogel hot ken Fligel, ken Feddre un ken Schnavel? (*Mortervogel.*)

What bird has no wings, no feathers, and no bill? (Hod; mortar bird.)

Was fer Eppel wachsa net uf Beem? (*Maiappel.*)

What kind of apples do not grow on trees? (May apples.)

Was fer Stee hots es menscht im Wasser? (*Nasse.*)

What kind of stones does one usually find in the water? (Wet stones.)

Was steht uf em Fuss urr hots Herz im Kop? (*Kraut Kop.*)

What stands on its foot and has its heart in its head? (Cabbagehead.)

Was wachst uf seim Schwantz? (*Rüb.*)

What grows on its own tail? (Turnip.)

Was hots Hertz im ganze Leib? (*En Baum.*)

What has its heart in its whole body? (A tree.)

Wer war gebore un is net gesterve? (*Du und feil annere.*)

Who was born but never died? (You and many others.)

Wann is en Fuchs en Fuchs? (*Wann er alee is, wann es zwee sin, sins Füchs.*)

When is a fox a fox? (When he is alone.)

A Connecticut Riddle Tale

A slave girl was told by her master that if she proposed a riddle he could not solve in seven days she should be free. In the woods she came upon a wren setting on a nest of five eggs in the skeleton of a horse and she made the following riddle. Her master could not solve it.

> As I walked out and in again
> From the dead the living came.
> Five there were, six there'll be,
> And seven shall set this maiden free.

Riddles from South Carolina

"Fry me some eggs, fry me some eggs!"
"Got no lard, got no lard!"
"Tallow will do, tallow will do."
"Cloddy land, cloddy land."
"Plough it deep, plough it deep!"
"Muddy de water, muddy de water!"

> (A pond full of green frogs talking to themselves. When the sixth frog says "Muddy de water," he see his enemy, they all disappear.)

If he come, he no come.
If he no come, he come.

> (Planted corn. If the crow come, corn no come.)

Green Morocco built a ship,
An' he built it for his daughter,
An' I've told her name three times,
An' I'm ashamed to tell three times over.
                    (Her name was Ann.)

    Clink, clank, under the bank,
    Ten against four.
            (The cow being milked.)

Up chip cherry, down chip cherry,
Many man in jerry
Can climb chip cherry.

                    (The sun.)

    Hitty titty in the house,
    Hitty titty out of doors,
    Nary man can catch hitty titty.
                    (Smoke.)

Riddles from South Carolina, with Variants

        Hands full,
        House full,
        Still can't ketch a spoonful.
                    (Smoke.)

Goes all the way 'round the house,
An' don't ketch but a spoonful.
                    (Smoke.)

All way 'roun' de house,
Come to de do' an' can't come in.
                    (Path.)

    Som't'in' goes all up to yer do'
    An' never goes in.

                    (Path.)

Go to the spring
An' never drink a drop.
(Path.)

Go by de spring
An' never duh drink.
(Path.)

Roun' as a saucer
An' deep as a cup,
No king horses
Can't pull it up.
(Well.)

Round as a saucer,
Deep as a saucer,
Three legs, cannot run.
Two ears an' cannot hear.
(Watch pocket.)

Round as a biscuit,
Busy as a bee,
Pretties' little thing
Ever did see.
(Watch.)

Round as a biscuit,
Round as a cup,
Black as ink,
Can't see a wink.
(Spider [skillet].)

Roun' as a biscuit,
Slick as a mole,
Long tail,
An' a thumb in hole.
(Frying pan.)

Round as a biscuit,
Deep as a well,
Got many winders as a hotel.
(Thimble.)

Round as a dollar,
Busy as a bee,
In the middle
Go tick, tack, tee!
(Watch.)

Onct I was goin' 'cross London Bridge.
Met a man,
I drunked his blood,
An' t'rowed his hide away.
(Watermelon.)

As I was going over London Bridge,
I met old Dr. Gray.
I sucked his blood,
An' threw his skin away.
(Watermelon.)

As I was goin' down de street,
I met with ol' gran'father.
I ate his meat an' drank his blood,
An' threw his hide away.
(Watermelon.)

One day I was going 'cross London Bridge,
An' met ol' lady Nancy.
Sucked her blood,
An' lef' her body dancin'.
(I picked a blackberry, an'
left de bush a-shakin'.)

As I was going across London Bridge,
I met Sister Sally Ann.
She was drunk, and I was sober,
So I kicked her over.
(A bottle of whiskey.)

Riddles from Louisiana

Thirty white horses
On a red hill.
Now they tramp, now they romp,
Now they stand still.

(Teeth and gum.)

As crooked as a ram's horn,
Teeth like a cat.
Guess all your lifetime,
You will never guess that.

(Brier bush.)

Rough on the outside,
Smooth within;
Nothing can enter
But a big flat thing.
When it enters,
It wiggles about,
And that is the time
The goodie comes out.

(Oyster.)

A riddle, a riddle, as I suppose:
A hundred eyes and never a nose.

(Sifter.)

Four legs up and four legs down,
Soft in the middle, and hard all 'round.

(Bed.)

Long big black fellow,
Pull the trigger, make it bellow—Bang!

(Gun.)

Riddles from New Jersey

Round as a ring,
Deep as a cup,
And all the king's mule teams
Can't pull it up.
        (A well dug in a hole.)

Chip chip cherry,
No man can climb
Chip chip cherry.
        (Smoke.)

What is a:
    Long slim black feller,
    When you pull his cock oh how it'll beller?
        (It's a gun.)

Ozark Mountain Riddles

Runs an' runs an' never walks,
Great long tongue an' never talks.
        (A wagon.)

Two heads, cain't talk,
Four legs, cain't walk,
Five ribs an' a backbone.
        (A flax break.)

Riddledy, riddledy, riddledy rout,
Whut does a leetle boy hold in his hand
When he goes out?
        (The doorpin.)

Down in th' dark dungeon
Thar sets a brave knight,
All bridled, all saddled,
All ready t' fight;
Call me his name for th' brass o' my bow,
I've told you three times now
An' still you don't know!

(The knight's name is All.)

White all over, black all over,
Red all over—whut is it?

(A newspaper.)

My face is marked,
My hands a-movin',
No time t' play,
Got t' run all day!

(A clock.)

Crooked as a rainbow,
Teeth like a cat,
I bet a gold fiddle
You cain't guess that!

(A green brier.)

Whut won't go up th' chimney up,
But will go up th' chimney down?
Whut won't go down th' chimney up,
But will go down th' chimney down?

(An umbrella.)

In a big red cave thar's a leetle white fence. It don't never rain on th' leetle white fence, but still it's allus wet. Whut is it? (A feller's teeth.)

A Blue Ridge Mountain Riddle

Hits as round as a ring
And as deep as the spring
And all the king's horses
Couldn't pull it up.

Round as a hoop
And deep as a cup
All the king's horses
Can't pull it up.

Round as a ring
And deep as a cup
All the king's horses
Can't pull it up.

(Well.)

Riddles from Tennessee

It grows in the woods; it bellows in towns;
If you guess this riddle, I'll give you five pounds.

(A fiddle.)

I don't have it and I don't want it,
And if I had it, I wouldn't take a million dollars for it.

(Bald head.)

Two ducks in front of two ducks,
Two ducks behind two ducks,
Two ducks between two ducks,
How many ducks are there?

(Four.)

It goes all over hills and plains
But when it comes to a river, it breaks its neck.

(A path.)

It goes all over the hills, but doesn't eat,
It goes to the creek, but doesn't drink.

(A cowbell.)

It goes in dry and comes out wet,
It tickles your stomach and makes you sweat.

(A washboard.)

What is it that goes up a tree and down a tree,
Has eyes and can't see?

(A button.)

All over the hills and back home at night,
Sits under the bed and gapes for bones.

(Shoes.)

It can run, and it can walk,
It has a tongue and can't talk.

(A wagon.)

Four legs and four eyes,
It can't walk and can't see.

(A stove.)

Black we are but much admired,
Men seek for us till they are tired,
We tire the horses, but comfort man;
Tell me this riddle if you can.

(Lumps of coal.)

In marble walls as white as milk,
Lined with a skin of softest silk,
Within a fountain crystal clear
A golden apple doth appear;
No doors there are to this stronghold
Yet things break in and steal the gold.

(An egg.)

As I was going over Westminister Bridge,
I met with a Westminister scholar;
He pulled off his cap and drew off his glove,
And wished me a very good morrow.
What is his name?

(Andrew.)

Riddles from Arkansas

What is it that gets longer if you take some off at either end? (A ditch.)

Lots of them go to the spring but none of 'em ever drink. (Footprints.)

What is bought by the yard and worn by the foot? (A carpet.)

What is it that takes in green, comes out white, and then turns yellow? (A cow; grass is green, milk is white, butter is yellow.)

Two hookers, two snookers,
Two lookers,
Four dilly-danders,
Four stiff-standers,
Two flip-flops,
One fling-by.
    (A cow; with horns, nostrils,
    eyes, teats, legs, ears, and
    tail.)

The man who made me, never used me.
The man who bought me, never used me.
The man who used me, never saw me.

(A coffin.)

What is the difference between the Prince of Wales, a papa gorilla, and a bald head? (The first is an heir apparent; the second is a hairy parent; the third is no hair apparent.)

GAMES

Games today are essentially forms of pastime and amusement. However, we must remember that what is a serious pursuit or a functional activity in one time and place may be but a game in another. The farmer who protects his henhouse and the gentleman who rides to the hounds are both out to destroy the fox.

The definition of games must include recognition that they are essentially dramatic, play contests. A game must involve more than one participant and the elements of struggle and climax. Usually there is a winner and a loser. Always there must be rules, spelled out or tacitly understood by the participants.

Almost all peoples have games, and few have a greater variety than the Anglo-American peoples. Folklorists have been particularly fascinated with the literary by-products of children's games involving jump-rope and ball-bouncing rhymes, partly because these chants offer an excellent opportunity to study the process of oral variation and partly because they retain so many vestiges of earlier times. Charles Francis Potter, for example, showed that "Eeny, Meeny, Minie, Mo" retains elements of Cymric shepherd counts, Latin, French Canadian, and American pre-Civil War political matter.

A fascinating offshoot of certain children's games is the play party, which replaced the square dance as a form of adult entertainment in areas where the fiddle was considered sinful, the waist swing too intimate, and dancing sacrilegious. Based on singing games that stress marching, skipping, and handswings, the play party borrowed heavily from the square dance for its formulas and vocal accompaniment. Called by various names, "evening party," "flang party," "gin-around," it revived and developed a whole body of texts and tunes that have come to be as well known as any of our folk music. "Pig in the Parlor," "Quebec Town," and "Rose in the Garden" all served their time in the play parties of our first settlers. In many communities, these dancing games were the main form of entertainment.

The best general studies of children's games are those by Peter and Iona Opie, particularly their standard work, *The Lore and Language of Schoolchildren* (Oxford, 1959). The essay by Jerome Fried in *The Standard Dictionary of Folklore, Mythology, and Legend,* Volume I (New York, 1949) and *American Nonsinging Games* (Norman, Okla., 1953) by Paul G. Brewster will serve as excellent introductions to the whole area, as will Benjamin A. Botkin's *American Play-Party Song* (Lincoln, Nebr., 1937) to the play party itself.

Woskate Takapsice or Sioux Shinney

Takapsice is an ancient gambling game played by men, and is their roughest and most athletic game. They often received serious wounds, or had their bones broken while playing it, but serious quarrels seldom resulted.

It may be played by a few or by hundreds, and formerly was played for a wager. The wager on important games was often very large; men, women, and children betting, sometimes all they possessed, or a band of Indians contributing to a bet to make it equal to that offered by another band.

In former times one band of Indians would challenge another to play this game. If the challenge was accepted they would camp together, and play for days at a time, making a gala time of it, giving feasts, dancing, and having a good time generally.

The implements used in the game are: *cantakapsice,* the club; *tapatakapsice,* the ball.

The club was made of an ash or choke-cherry sapling, taken in the spring when the sap was running, and heated in the fire until it was pliable, when the lower end was bent until it stood at right angles to the rest of the stick, or into a semicircular crook, about six inches across.

The shape of this crook varied to suit the fancy of the maker.

After the crook was made, the stick was trimmed down to a uniform diameter of about one and a half inches, and cut of such a length that the player could strike on the ground with it while standing erect.

Anyone might make a club, but certain persons were supposed to make clubs of superior excellence, and some persons were supposed to be able to confer magical powers on clubs, causing the possessor to exercise unusual skill in playing. These magic clubs were supposed to be potent, not only in games, but to work enchantment in all kinds of affairs, for or against a person, as the possessor chose. The medicine men sometimes included such clubs among their paraphernalia, and invoked their magic powers in their incantations over the sick.

Certain medicine men were supposed to have the power to make medicine over clubs, so that any one in whose favor this medicine was made, by carrying it and the club during the game for which the medicine was made, would be on the winning side.

One possessing a magic club boasted of it, and the matter was generally known, but one who had medicine made over a club must keep the matter secret, for a general knowledge of the existence of the medicine would either destroy its potency, or others knowing of the medicine might have a more powerful medicine made against it, or the magic of a talisman could be exercised especially against it, and defeat its power.

A player who possessed a magic club was feared by those who did not, and the latter tried to avoid coming in contact with such a club while playing the game. This gave the possessors of such clubs decided advantages over others, and they were eagerly sought as players, and heavy wagers laid on their playing.

The clubs were generally without ornament, but they were sometimes ornamented by pyrographic figures on the handle or body. Certain clubs were highly prized by their owners, who took great care of them, frequently oiling and polishing them.

When a club was held for its magic power alone, as by the medicine men, it was often highly ornamented with feathers, bead work, porcupine quills, or tufts of hair.

The ball was made by winding some material into a ball, and covering it with buckskin or rawhide, or of wood. It was from two and a half to three inches in diameter.

The game is played where two goals can be set up with a level track of land between them.

The rules of the game are:

Any number of men may play, but there must be an equal number on the opposing sides.

In a series of games the same persons must play in each game of the series.

After the game begins, if any player stops playing, a player from the opposing party must stop playing also.

The players of a game must fix the goals before beginning to play.

Each of the two goals must consist of two stakes set about fifty to one hundred feet apart, and a line drawn from one stake to the other, which must be nearly parallel to the line drawn at the other goal.

The goals must be from three hundred yards to one mile apart, as may be agreed upon between the players, for each game.

After the goals are fixed the players choose their goal, either by agreement or by lot.

After the goals are chosen the players arrange themselves in two lines, about half way between the goals, all the players on one side standing in one line, and each side facing the goal it has chosen, the lines being about thirty feet apart.

After the players are in line the ball is placed as nearly as can be half way between them.

After the ball is placed on the ground it must not be touched by the hand or foot of any one until the game is ended.

If at any time during the play the ball becomes so damaged that it is unfit for use, the game is called off, and another game must be played to decide the contest.

The club may be used in any manner to make a play, or to prevent an opponent from making a play.

After the ball is placed on the ground, at a given signal, each side attempts to put the ball across its goal in a direction opposite from the other goal.

The side that first puts the ball across its goal in the proper direction wins the game.

The King's Army

We have in this game an echo of the Revolutionary War. The game seems also to be the child's adaptation of the old English game of Tug-of-War. It is played thus: two children separate from the others, and each selects a name for himself; it may be anything, but as I find it sometimes played, one child selects the name Tory and the other Whig, without letting the other children know which is which. These two leaders then face each other joining hands, while the others form in column, and as they approach the two, all sing:

> Hoist the gates as high as the sky,
> And let King George's army pass by.

The two raise their clasped hands, and the army marches triumphantly under; all pass except the last one, upon whom the raised arms suddenly fall, unless he is so agile as to escape by ducking and dodging. If he is caught the column marches on and the captive is asked in a whisper if he is a Whig or a Tory. The column approaches the gate again, and the same formula is repeated; this is kept up until the whole army is captured, one by one, and is lined up, part behind the Whig and part behind the Tory, sometimes of course with a very unequal division. Then each little fellow clasps the one in front of him around the waist, and, at a word from the leaders, who still tightly clasp hands, every child pulls with all his might, the object being to pull down the opposing side.

A Game with Eggs on Easter

During Lent, and especially on Easter Sunday, the Syrians have a custom of playing with eggs. The game is as follows: two persons take a number of eggs apiece, testing them upon their teeth to get as strong-shelled ones as possible. The sharper end is called the head, and the other the heel. Then A says, "With my head I will break your head," or, if he thinks he has a very hard-shelled egg, he may say, "With my head I will break your head and your heel too." B may then make the threat to take A's egg and with its heel break both ends of his own egg. But suppose he does not, and the game goes on with A's threat to B. B then wraps his hand tightly about the egg and, leaving only the very tip exposed, says, "Well, break it!" A says, "You are not showing very much of it." B then moves his hand down a trifle, and A, if he thinks he can break it, strikes. But if he thinks that he cannot break it, he says, "I will show you more than that," and takes B's egg and gives B his egg. B then does the striking, and if he succeeds in breaking A's egg he wins it. If, on the contrary, B's egg is broken by the blow, A wins it. The one who loses then produces a new egg, and the game continues until the supply of either one or the other is exhausted.

A Counting Game

A girl holds out her apron with one hand and all her companions take hold of the edge of the apron with two fingers of each hand. The girl thereupon recites the rhymes, one line for each hand, moving her fingers from right to left.

The hand which is touched at the last line . . . must be withdrawn.

> *Minzin Minzol*
> *Cazim Cazol,*
> *Por mor de ti*
> *José Manzol.*
> *Cascaranhas,*
> *Tringue lá forá.*

TRANSLATION:

> Minzin Minzol
> Cazim Cazol,
> For love of thee,
> José Manzol.
> They will break them,
> Break them there outside.

A Rapid Counting Contest

This verse is recited in contests of rapid counting by children in Lower California, Mexico. It seems to have originated in Spain because the *bota*, which is the name of a leather jug used to carry wine in Spain, is not used in Mexico.

Una—dále vuelta a la luna	One—go around the moon
Dos—dále cuerda al reloj	Two—wind the clock
Tres—la mano del almirez	Three—the pestle of the mortar
Cuatro—come en tu plato	Four—eat in your plate
Cinco—pégale un brinco	Five—jump over it
Seis—dále al revés	Six—hurl it away
Siete—dále un moquete	Seven—give it a blow
Ocho—cómete un bizcocho	Eight—eat a cake

Nueve—alza la bota y bebe	Nine—raise the wineskin and drink
Diez—álzala otra vez	Ten—raise it again
Once—cucharón de bronce	Eleven—dipper of bronze
Doce—tírate un pedo y acabose.	Twelve—make a noise [?] and it is finished.

A Mexican Ring Game

This refrain is chanted over and over by children in Lower California as they hold hands going around and around in a circle until someone falls.

A la rueda del garbanzo	At the chick pea wheel
El que se cae es burro manso.	The one who falls is a tame donkey.

The Little Coyote

One child acts as mother, and leads the children around another child who sits in the center, and represents the coyote. The mother and children pinch coyote in the head, and say:

> *Pepenando piñoncitos,*
> *pepenando piñoncitos,*
> *para el pobre coyotito,*
> *para el pobre coyotito.*
> Etc.

> Picking piñon nuts,
> picking piñon nuts,
> for the poor little coyote,
> for the poor little coyote.
> Etc.

The coyote finally becomes angry and catches one of the children.

In another coyote game, the children come out as before and say:

> —*Mira la luna.*
> [Coyote looks at the moon.]
> —*M, m, m. ¡Qué piojero!*
> [Then all scream:]
> —*Salta, coyote,*
> *con tanto majote.*
> [Coyote runs away.]

> Look at the moon.
> M, m, m. What lice!
> Jump, coyote,
> As handsomely as you can.

A Guessing Game with Pecans

One person holds several pecans in his hand and says, *"Ti zozo dan boi."* ("Little bird in the bush.") The other replies, *"Tiré li."* ("I'll hit [guess] it [this one].") *"Combien coups?"* ("How many times?") *"Dé, trois, cate"* ("Two, three, four"), etc. If the player has guessed right, he wins the pecans; otherwise he must give the same number of nuts to his adversary.

Club Fist

A matching-up game called "Club fist," which resembles the choosing-up method in sand-lot baseball, is started by each player putting his fist on top of that of the previous player until each has a fist in the stack. Then "It" says to the player who has his fist on the top:

"What you got there?" "Club fist." "Well, take it off or
I'll knock it off."

And so each fist is removed until the last one, when
the following exchange of questions and answers takes
place: It: "What you got there?" Player: "Piece of cheese."
"Where's my share?" "Cat got it." "Where's the cat?" "In
the woods." "Where're the woods?" "Fire burned it."
"Where's the fire?" "Water squenched it." "Where's the
water?" "Ox drank it." "Where's the ox?" "Butcher killed
it." "Where's the butcher?" "Rope hung him." "Where's
the rope?" "Rat gnawed it." "Where's the rat?" "Cat caught
him." "Where's the cat?" "Dead and buried behind the
church door, and now the first one who shows his teeth
gets ten pinches and ten rousing boxes."

Then "It" tries to make the other players laugh or speak.

Ring Games of Negro Children

Good Old Egg-bread

The leader shouts one line, and the others answer with
the next. The rhythm is very strong, and they stamp their
feet most energetically as they circle.

> Did you go to the henhouse?
>   Yes, ma'am!
> Did you get any eggs?
>   Yes, ma'am!
> Did you put 'em in the bread?
>   Yes, ma'am!
> Did you stir it 'roun'?
>   Yes, ma'am!
> Did you bake it brown?
>   Yes, ma'am!
> Did you hand it 'roun'?
>   Yes, ma'am!

Good old egg-bread,
   Shake 'em, shake 'em!
Good old egg-bread,
   Shake 'em, shake 'em!

Did you go to the lynchin'?
   Yes, ma'am!
Did they lynch that man?
   Yes, ma'am!
Did the man cry?
   Yes, ma'am!
How did he cry?
   Baa, baa!
How did he cry?
   Baa, baa!

Did you go to the wedding?
   Yes, ma'am!
Did you get any wine?
   Yes, ma'am!
Did you get any cake?
   Yes, ma'am!
How did it taste?
   So good!
How did it taste?
   So good!
Good old egg-bread,
   Shake 'em, shake 'em!
Good old egg-bread,
   Shake 'em, shake 'em!
Bow, Mr. Blackbird, bow, Mr. Crow.
Bow, Mr. Blackbird, bow no mo'!

WAY DOWN YONDER

Way down yonder
  Soup to soup!
Where dem white folks
  Soup to soup!
Just singin' an' prayin'
  Soup to soup!
Tryin' to make man
  Soup to soup!
Biscuits hot
  Soup to soup!
Corn bread cold
  Soup to soup!
Thank God Almighty
  Soup to soup!
Just give me a little mo'
  Soup to soup!

TAKE YOUR LOVER IN THE RING

My old mistress promised me
Before she died she would set me free.
  Take your lover in the ring.
    I don't care!
  Take your lover in the ring.
    I don't care!
Now she's dead and gone to hell.
I hope that devil will burn her well!
  Take your lover in the ring.
    I don't care!
  Take your lover in the ring.
    I don't care!
  It's a golden ring.
    I don't care!
  It's a silver ring.
    I don't care!

Quebec Town

The following contains a memory of the Revolutionary
War:

> We are marching down to Quebec town,
> Where the drums and fifes are beating;
> The Americans have gained the day,
> And the British are retreating.
> The war's all over; we'll turn back
> To friends, no more to be parted.
> We'll open our ring and receive another in
> To relieve this broken-hearted.

The manner of playing was as follows: the song was
sung by the whole company, as it marched around one
person, who was blindfolded, and seated in a chair placed
in the center of the room. He or she then selected a partner by touching one of the ring with a long stick held for
the purpose. The game concluded:

> Put a hat on her head to keep her head warm,
> And a loving, sweet kiss will do her no harm.

An Evening Party Song-Game

[Song-games] were played and sung in the back country
towns of Connecticut as late as the year 1870, at the so-
called "Evening Party." In the center of the house was
usually found a large and old chimney, and the rooms
were connected by doors, so that it was possible to march
round. In each cosy corner was stationed one to choose
from the players, who moved marching and singing; at
the proper time in the game the chooser took a sounding
kiss, and left his choice to continue in the same manner.
About midnight were passed refreshments of several kinds,
"frosted cake," apples, popped corn, walnuts and butter-
nuts already cracked, a pitcher of cider, and another of

cold water; no napkins were thought of. Each guest was seated and given an empty plate, after which the young men handed the good things on large waiters. The singing and marching was resumed, and kept up until about four o'clock in the morning, when the young men issued and huddled about the door, and as the girls came out, each stepped forward, and offered his arm to his choice, with the words: "Can I see you home?" after which they separated, and went in the dark, often across fields, to their scattered homes, perhaps two miles away; at the door of the fair one (which often was the back door, when snow lay on the ground, and no path had been shoveled to the front entrance), there was always a final hug and kiss.

ROSE IN THE GARDEN

Sail- ing in the boat when the tide runs high,

Sail - ing in the boat when the tide runs high,

Sail - ing in the boat when the tide runs high,

Wait - ing for the pret - ty girl to come by'm by.

Here she comes so fresh and fair, Sky- blue eyes and curl - y hair,

Ro- sy in cheek, dimple in her chin, Say, young men, but you can't come in.

Sailing in the boat when the tide runs high,
Sailing in the boat when the tide runs high,
Sailing in the boat when the tide runs high,
Waiting for the pretty girl to come by 'm by.
Here she comes so fresh and fair,
Sky-blue eyes and curly hair,
Rosy in cheek, dimple in her chin,
Say, young men, but you can't come in.

Rose in the garden for you, young man,
Rose in the garden for you, young man,
Rose in the garden, get it if you can,
But take care and don't get a frost-bitten one.

Choose your partner, stay till day,
Choose your partner, stay till day,
Choose your partner, stay till day,
Never, never mind what the old folks say.

Old folks say 't is the very best way,
Old folks say 't is the very best way,
Old folks say 't is the very best way,
To court all night and sleep all day.

Snap

One of the most popular games at the parties [in the Ozark mountains] at which we have disported ourselves is called "Snap," and begins with one boy and one girl standing in the center of the room. This boy and girl face each other, hold hands, and brace themselves so as not to be separated or upset by people running into them. The other players sit around the sides of the room, leaving a clear space about the couple in the center. A boy is usually the first "It," and he walks about the room, finally snapping his fingers in a girl's face. The girl who has been "snapped" chases the boy round and round the standing couple, with much dodging and twisting and bumping into one another, so that it often happens that all four fall in a heap. When the girl catches the boy who snapped her, he takes the place of the boy who was standing; then the girl who caught him snaps her fingers in a boy's face, and is chased in her turn. When she is caught, she changes places with the girl who has been standing all this time, and so it goes. "Snap" is rather a rough and rowdy game, often characterized by a great display of lingerie or the lack of it.

A Ball-Bouncing Game

These numbers and rhymes were chanted as an accompaniment to bouncing a rubber ball. The children of my generation [ca. 1895] recited the numbers through twenty-four, but the children who played this game on the St. Louis playgrounds in 1914 had increased the number to nearly a hundred.

> One, two, button my shoe;
> Three, four, shut the door;
> Five, six, pick up sticks;
> Seven, eight, lay them straight;
> Nine, ten, the big fat hen;
> Eleven, twelve, mind yourself;
> Thirteen, fourteen, maids are sporting;
> Fifteen, sixteen, maids are kissing;
> Seventeen, eighteen, maids are waiting;
> Nineteen, twenty, maids are plenty;
> Twenty-one, twenty-two,
> If you love me as I love you,
> No knife can cut our love in two;
> Twenty-three, twenty-four,
> Mary at the kitchen door,
> Eating apples by the score,
> One, two, three, four.

A Ball-Bouncing and Rope-Jumping Song

> Hello! Hello, sir!
> Meet me at the grocer.
> No, sir! Why, sir?
> Because I have a cold, sir.
> Where did you get the cold, sir?
> At the North Pole, sir.
> What were you doing there, sir?
> Catching polar bears, sir.
> How many did you catch, sir?
> One, sir; two, sir; [etc., until]
> Ten, sir.
> Old Dutch Cleanser.

Jump-Rope Rhymes

There are various types of jingles to go with the different games:

> Gypsy, Gypsy, please tell me,
> What my husband's first initial will be.

At this point the girls start repeating the alphabet and when the correct letter is reached the girl jumps out.

Jumping rope has become something of an endurance test, as is evidenced by the following:

> Grace, Grace, monkey face,
> Went upstairs to powder her face.
> How many boxes did she use?
> One, two, three, etc.

Five little girls co-ordinate this number, and jump to this jingle:

> All in together girls,
> Very fine weather girls,
> When is your birthday girls,
> January, February, March,
> April, etc.

They jump "out" when the month of their birthday is reached, and then they repeat the jingle but substitute the day and date in place of the month.

Another for jumping rope is:

Peel a banana upside down,
Peel an orange round and round
If you count to twenty-one,
You shall have another turn.
Not last night but the night before,
Three little gents came knocking at my door.
I got up to let them in,
And what do you suppose they began to sing!
Lady, lady, lady, turn around, 'round, 'round.
Lady, lady, lady, touch the ground, ground, ground.
Lady, lady, lady, tie your shoe, shoe, shoe.
Lady, lady, lady, please skeedo, skeedo, skeedo.

A Political Jump-Rope Rhyme

Down in the valley where the green grass grows,
There sits Kennedy as sweet as a rose.
Along came Nixon and kissed him on the cheek.
How many kisses did he receive?
One, two, three, four, etc.

Counting Out Rhymes, with Variants

ONE, TWO, THREE

One potato, two potato, three potato, four,
Five potato, six potato, seven potato o'er.

One, two, three,
The bumblebee.
The rooster crows,
And away she goes.

One, two, three, four,
Nellie at the cottage door,
Giving cherries to the poor.
One, two, three, four.

One, two, three, four, five,
I caught a hen alive;
Six, seven, eight, nine, ten,
I let her go again.

One, two, three, four, five, six, seven,
All good children go to Heaven;
Penny on the water,
Tuppence on the sea,
Threepence on the railway;
Out goes she.

One, two, three, four, five, six, seven,
All good children go to Heaven.
Some go up, and some go down,
And some go to the burying ground.

One, two, three, four, five, six, seven,
All good children go to Heaven.
When they get there, they will shout,
O-u-t, and that spells out.

ONE-ERY, TWO-ERY

One-ery, two-ery, ickery, Ann.
Fillacy, fallacy, Nicholas Zann;
Queevy, quavy, Irish Navy.
Stingalum, stangalum, buck.

Erie, Irie, Ickery, Ann,
Phyllis, Phallus, Nicholas, John.
Queever, quaver, English neighbor,
Stringilum, strangilum, Roe Buck.

Ury, Iry, Ichery, Jam,
Phillisy, Phollosy, Nicholas John,
Queby, Quoby, English Mary.
Stickilum, Stackelum,
Wee, Woe, Buck.

A Children's Dance Rhyme

A circle having been formed, the children move slowly, singing as follows:

Mamma bought me a pincushion, pincushion, pincushion,
Mamma bought me a pincushion,
   One, two, three.

At the words, "One, two, three," the children break the circle; each claps hands and turns once round. (This movement appears to make the charm of the game.) The song then proceeds, with repetition, as in the first stanza:

What did Mamma pay for it?
Paid with Papa's feather bed.
What will Papa sleep on?
Sleep on the washtub.
What will Mamma wash in?

Wash in a thimble.
What will Mamma sew with?
Sew with a poker.
What will Mamma poke with?
Poke with her finger.
Supposing Mamma burns herself?

Hop Scotch

Two distinct ways of playing this game exist among the children of Brooklyn: one common among boys and girls, called "Kick the stone out," and another, said to be played exclusively by girls, called "Pick the stone up." In the former a diagram, as shown in the figure, is drawn upon the sidewalk, where five flagstones, as nearly of a size as possible, are selected, of which the second and fourth are divided in halves by a line drawn vertically through the center. The compartment formed by the entire surface of the first stone is marked 1; the two compartments on the next stone, 2 and 3; the third stone is marked 4; the fourth stone, 5 and 6; and the fifth and last stone, "home." The diagram may be enlarged, and the numbers continued up to 10, which makes the game longer and more difficult. Each player finds a stone of convenient size, one about an inch thick being usually selected.

home	
5	6
4	
2	3
1	

The first player stands without the diagram, and throws his stone into the compartment marked 1. If it falls fairly within that compartment, he hops on one foot into the same place and kicks the stone out, taking care not to put down his other foot or to step on a dividing line, as either would lose him his turn. If he succeeds in kicking the stone out and hopping out himself, he throws the stone into number 2, and then hops into number 1, and from that into number 2, kicks the stone out, and hops back as before. This is continued until "home" is reached, and the one arriving there first wins the game. "Pick the stone up" is played in the same manner as "Kick the stone out," except that the players pick the stone up instead of kicking it out.

FOLK DRAMA AND FOLK FESTIVAL

There are very few folk dramas to be found in American oral tradition. Excepting a few survivals of Christmas plays in the southern mountains, the miracle plays still performed in Mexico and the Mexican-American Southwest, and the mimic matter associated with festivals, drama that has been handed down traditionally from generation to generation is, and has been for a long time, rare. The explanation for its rarity is not hard to uncover. Drama in western Europe, as in most places, grew from church ceremonies, rituals, and festivals. The Church in the Middle Ages was the center of literacy and its tendency was toward literary composition and record. Then, too, the flowering of western European drama coincides roughly with the growth of printing, and plays were often printed because it was difficult to preserve them without the aid of transcription of some sort. It takes a whole community to recall all the parts of a play that survives orally, each role being handed down in a separate tradition. Thus, even allowing for a central, transcribed text of the entire play, the chances of survival for drama at the folk level are far less than for a simple ballad or folktale or even an epic.

However, rare as true folk drama is, much of folklore is inherently dramatic. Tales are dramatized, ballads become dance games, games become playlets. For instance, quite a number of Negro groups in the West Indies and in the southern states have dramatized the singing of the ballad "The Maid Freed from the Gallows," a practice not too different from the dramatization of Robin Hood ballads that characterizes the English May-day festivals. The folk are quick to capitalize on dramatic potentiality.

Nowhere is this more true than in the folk festival, where ancient rituals, many of them once associated with agricultural rites no longer understood, are revived and re-enacted year after year in communities across the land. Such rituals are never static. They change, add matter from recent times, mix cultures, end up as conglomerations of this and that in a way that reflects the polyglot world we live in. Among the most famous American festivals are the Philadelphia Mummers Parade, the New Orleans Mardi Gras, and the French *La Guillannée*.

There is no adequate study of folk drama and folk festival in America. However, Juan B. Rael's *The Sources and Diffusion of the Mexican Shepherd's Plays* (Guadalajara, Mexico, 1965) is an excellent starting point for the study of Mexican-American material, while Edmund K. Chambers, *The Medieval Stage* (Oxford, 1954) is a fundamental general work.

One should be careful not to confuse works such as those included in Frederick Koch's *Carolina Folk-Plays* (New York, 1941), for example the plays of Paul Green, with authentic folk drama. *Carolina Folk-Plays* and the like are created by highly trained artists and have never been in oral tradition.

A Miracle Play of the Rio Grande

The *locus* of the play ["Los Pastores"] is supposed to be Palestine, and the *dramatis personæ* include, besides the Holy Mother and Babe—whose presence, however, in our days is suggested rather than revealed, as a *présibi*, or manger, is generally erected, before which the actors stand —a Chorus of Shepherds and Shepherdesses, a Head Shepherd, Michael the Archangel, Lucifer and several of his Imps, and an aged *Ermitaño,* or Hermit, whose life has been passed in devout contemplation, and who now, bent with age and hoary of beard, admonishes and advises the ignorant herders who resort to him for spiritual consolation.

There are several rather ludicrous incongruities which may be recognized without giving offense to the pious fervor of the actors and actresses, who become intensely wrought up in their parts as the plot unfolds. The Hermit carries, attached to his waist, a rosary made of wooden spools, and bears in his right hand a large crucifix, although the Saviour has not yet been born and his Passion is all yet to be undergone. In every case that I saw or heard of, the rosary was made of these large wooden spools.

Whenever it could be conveniently done, Lucifer was dressed in the uniform of a cavalry officer, but time is working changes, and at this writing his Satanic Majesty enacts his role in raiment not so pronouncedly martial.

For weeks beforehand the actors selected meet under the superintendence of the Head Shepherd (in the present case an intelligent cobbler), and listen attentively and patiently while he reads, line by line and word by word, the part of each. Very few of them can read or write, and none of them in a manner betokening extensive practice; the dependence for success, therefore, is almost wholly

upon eye, ear, and memory, and the rehearsals are repeated again and again, until every man, woman, and child
can recite the lines almost mechanically.

The Shepherds and Shepherdesses are in gala dress, and
provided with elaborately decorated *ganchos,* or crooks,
one of which may now be seen in the National Museum
at Washington. The Archangel Michael is distinguishable
by his wings and remorseless sword, as well as by the ran-
cor with which he at all times assails his old adversary,
the Son of the Morning. Both Michael and Lucifer rant a
little too much to satisfy critical taste, but allowance must
be made that the event they contemplate is the crucial
epoch in the life of mankind, and both are speaking to
influence suffrages in their favor.

There are ceaseless repetitions, and promenades and
countermarches without end or object, save, perhaps, to
allow each artist opportunity for a nasalized enunciation
of his verses, in chant or monologue.

The first rehearsal which I witnessed lasted over three
hours, and all the others nearly the same time, yet both
actors and audience maintained a stolid and dogged atten-
tion beyond all praise.

The music is inferior and the singing execrable, because the voices of the women and men of the Lower Rio
Grande are generally too attenuated and stridulous to be
pleasing; nevertheless there are occasional snatches of har-
mony which dwell agreeably in memory.

Unlike the theatrical and acrobatic representations, there
are no fixed charges for admission to the *Pastores;* those
who have money are expected to pay, and those who
have none are made welcome without it.

But, much after the manner of the Christmas carols of
Old England, the *Pastores* will gladly go from house to
house of the more wealthy, enacting their parts with all
due fervor, and expecting in return a largess of hospitality
and a small pittance in money.

The church of late years has set its face against the

appearance of the *Pastores* within the walls of sacred edi-
fices, but they are looked upon as innocent and harmless,
and free scope given them within their present circum-
scribed limits.

As the proof of the pudding is in the eating, it may be
well to let my readers form for themselves an idea of the
language and plot.

The libretto, containing between eight and ten thousand words, of which passages are given below, was written out for me by Francisco Collazo, the Head Shepherd.

The shepherds have just learned from the Archangel
Michael the glad tidings of great joy, and have burst out
in pæans of praise and gratitude:

> *En el portal de Belen*
> *Hay muy grande claridad,*
> *Porque allá nació el Mécias*
> *Y el nos pondrá en libertad.*

> In the Gate of Bethlehem
> There is great light,
> For there has been born the Messiah
> Who is to set us at liberty.

And so on through seven verses more, none of significance, excepting the one in which Gila, the Shepherdess,
is commanded by the Chief Shepherd to get ready plenty
of *tamales* for the subsistence of the shepherds during
their journey to Bethlehem. *Tamales,* it must be well
known, are one of the staple articles of diet of the Mexi-
cans, who have inherited them from the Aztecs, although
something similar may have been known in Spain and
Palestine.

Lucifer, called Luzbel in the libretto, now rushes upon
the scene and indulges in frenzied soliloquy: "Driven out
of heaven by the sword of Michael on account of proud
ambition and infamous crime, I boasted of my fault, for
the earth was still mine. But what is this I hear? These

songs of gladness—these victorious chants of seraphim?
What is this I hear of the Star newly seen in Arabia?"
Then he bethinks himself that the fulfillment of time is at
hand, the seventy weeks of Daniel have expired, and the
prophecies of Ezekiel are accomplished. In Bethlehem he
learns that in a manger oxen and asses have kept warm
with their breath a little babe whom his fears tell him only
too plainly is the Incarnate Word.

There is a very considerable amount of this soliloquy,
and it is evident to the most careless listener that Luzbel,
or Lucifer, is not at all pleased with the prospect opening
before him.

Seeing the band of shepherds and shepherdesses approaching the summit of the hill on which he had taken
his stand, he conceals himself to listen to their conversation, and no sooner is he hidden from the eyes of all but
the audience than the aged Hermit emerges from his seclusion to greet the procession.

Two of the shepherds—Parrado and Tebano—and Gila,
indulge in singing, telling what great presents of costly
stones and jewels they would make to the church, were
Fortune kind enough to bless them with abundant means.

We may indulge in the by no means violent conjecture
that the pious friar who prepared the original libretto,
back in Spain or the Canaries, fancied he saw an oppor-
tune moment for inspiring the spectators with proper
sentiments of duty towards Holy Mother Church.

Finally, Gila concludes these songs with the following:

> *Pastores, ya llégo el dia*
> *En que, alegres, nos partamos*
> *Para el Portal de Belen,*
> *A ver un feliz milagro.*
> *Compongan sus bastimientos,*
> *Y dispongan bien sus Latas.*
> *Caminemos gustosos,*
> *Festejandonos con cantos.*

Shepherds, the day is dawning
When joyfully we shall set out
For the Gate of Bethlehem,
To see a great miracle.
Get ready your food,
And arrange your clothes.
Joyfully we'll travel,
Solacing each other with song.

Then we are treated to a chorus of sixteen verses, one of which will be sufficient:

En risueños cantos,
De los ruiseñores,
Caminemos alegres,
Hermanos pastores.

With joyful songs,
Like those of nightingale,
Let's gladly march,
Brother shepherds.

They don't forget to take their sheep with them, a fact which is duly recorded in the verses. The Hermit addresses the shepherds, and is kindly received and made to eat of *cabrito* (goat meat), *pinole* (an Aztec dish), *tortillas*, and *tamales*.

One of the shepherd characters—Bartolo—is represented as lazy and gluttonous, always seeking an excuse for rest, instead of progressing on to Bethlehem. He furnishes whatever of the odd and ridiculous the situation may occasionally demand, while the impotent rage and utter discomfort of Lucifer border closely upon the comical, although they never lose all gravity and seriousness. It is almost time for another chorus, and we get it:

Esta si que es Noche Buena
De regocijo y amor,
Porque dicen que nació
El Divino Redentor.

This is truly the Good Night [Christmas]
Of joy and love,
Because they say
The Divine Redeemer is born.

More singing is indulged in by the shepherds, Bato, Bartolo, and Parrado, and the Sacred Babe is compared to Samson, Jonah, Solomon, Jesse, David, and Michael.

The Archangel now appears to Bartolo and says to him, "Gloria in excelsis," and repeats the news that Christ is born.

Bartolo awakens his comrades, who have been taking a siesta after their singing, and demands that they give him *albricias,* a kind of present which in old times in Spain was always bestowed upon the bearer of good news.

Michael, mingling with the pastoral throng, warns them that Lucifer is approaching, but bids them be of good cheer, that he will defend them.

Luzbel, or Lucifer, meekly advances, assures the shepherds that he is a poor wanderer, and beseeches shelter and food.

His new-found hosts do not like the great amount of black in his garments, or the lion's muzzle which forms his face. Lucifer endeavors to soothe them by saying that he is the richest man in the world, and anxious to share his *hacienda* (treasure) with them.

About this part of the miracle play there are some fine lines—those in which Lucifer alludes to his former pre-eminence and fall, and those in which Michael addresses him, although in these last is to be found another anach-ronism, that in which the Archangel says he will smite Lucifer with the potent name of Mary, who could hardly as yet have been recognized as the Mother of the Most High.

Lucifer implores Michael to leave him the dominion of the earth, which has so long been under his control.

This interview with Michael is an aside, and unperceived by the shepherds, who get ready to sup, and repeat as a grace a sort of burlesque upon the prayers of the monastic orders, which runs thus: *Nominis, santi, adentro, abiscum, pastores, canteis, cantice-flores.*

In this part of the work may be detected several solecisms and errors, the most noticeable of which, perhaps, is the word *ejemplador* for *imperador* (emperor), used by Lucifer in describing to the shepherds the wealth and power of his father. Michael also demands of Lucifer why he presumes to molest these "Christian" (!) shepherds in their pilgrimage.

The Infernal One is soon disposed of, and the shepherds find themselves in front of the manger of Bethlehem. There is a great increase in the number of hymns and prayers of adoration, each of the shepherds chanting a hymn and reciting a prayer while he deposits his gifts. Parrado expresses his surprise that the Holy Infant is so small, and hopes he may soon grow big enough to play with his (Parrado's) nephew, Andrecito.

The gifts are varied, but very cheap, and seem to consist mainly of flowers, bed linen, clothing, playthings, honey, food, and silver, which last is said to have been made by a *platero* (silversmith) from Mexico, a detail which enables us to fix the date of the composition as later than A.D. 1520.

Another circumstance, insignificant in itself, but of consequence in this connection, is that the shepherd Lizardo makes a present of *Holanda*, or Holland linen.

> *A la sombra de un' arbol frondosa,*
> *Esta la madre del Gran Redentor,*
> *Abreviada en su sombra descansa,*

Fatigada del grande dolor.
Y las aves con sonrosas voces,
La acarician y juegan con el.
Y el chiquito, llorando, la dice,
Oh maman! que fria es la nieve!
Camina, Señora, y no desmayais,
Que à Belen, dichosa, preste llegareis.

In the shade of a leafy tree
Lies the Mother of the Great Redeemer,
With scarcely any shelter,
Exhausted with great grief;
And the merry-voiced birds
Caress her and play with Him,
And the little one keeps saying,
"Oh, mamma, how cold the snow is!
Travel along, lady, and be not dismayed,
Because, happy one, soon you'll reach Bethlehem."

The final songs include one of the alphabet, in which each letter is credited with certain qualities, but exactly what all this means it would be hard to say.

Christmas Masking in Boston

When my mother was a girl (she was born about 1752, and died at the age of ninety-five years) maskers came to houses and entered with a prologue, each making a speech. The performance included a prologue, combat, cure, and questions. I remember the following lines:

> Here comes I who never came yet,
> Great head and little wit,
> And though my wit it is so ill,
> Before I go I'll please you still.

Next came questions and evasive answers:

"How wide is this river?"
"The ducks and the geese they do fly over."

The asker was a traveler coming over. All were maskers
in disguise, with swords, etc. At this time Christmas was
not kept.

A Mummers' Play from the Kentucky Mountains

THE CAST

The Presenter—not in costume.

Father Christmas—Santa Claus suit borrowed from the
school. Holly in his beard. Carried a frying pan and a
dead rabbit.

Dame Dorothy—A man dressed in bright colored woman's
clothes. Veil made of an old window curtain served as
a mask. Red paper pinned inside the front of her dress
was displayed later as blood.

Old Bet—A man dressed as an old woman. Apron, bonnet
and shawl. Mistletoe on bonnet.

The Bessie—A man dressed as a woman with a cow's tail
fastened on. Grotesque mask of brown paper with horns
sticking up. Holly on the horns. Carried two cowbells
strung across his hips.

Little Devil Doubt—A boy with his face blacked. A hump
on his back. Gay red paper streamers tied around his
arms and neck. Holly on his hat.

Pickle Herring—A man wearing a woman's "bedgown" under a man's overcoat. Carried an inflated pig's bladder
colored like a balloon. A dunce cap with gay streamers
served as a mask. Many floating red paper streamers.

Doctor Good—A man wearing a long-tailed coat, spectacles,
and a very high top hat. Face painted very red. No
other mask. Holly on his hat. Carried a doctor's bag.

Chorus—Eight high school boys wearing the white smocks

of the home economics class. Paper bags over their heads as masks. Holly wreaths around their necks.

According to Tom and George Fields [two of the actors] the following parts of the costuming were "fixed by the way the old time folks decked out to go mumming":

The red paper or cloth pinned inside Dame Dorothy's dress and used to represent blood.

The woman's clothing on Old Bet.

The cow's tail, the woman's clothing, and the cowbells on The Bessie.

The "bedgown," the dunce cap, and the inflated bladder for the Pickle Herring.

The professional garb and red painted face or red mask on Doctor Good.

The white smocks on the Chorus.

Holly, masks, and gay streamers on the cast. Other items of costuming were merely rustic attempts at disguise.

THE PLAY

(*After a huge bonfire has been made to give heat and light*)

PRESENTER: We air now aiming to give a dumb show for to pleasure the Little Teacher for not going off to the level country to keep Christmas with her kin. Hit ain't noways perfect the way we act out this here dumb show, but hit ain't been acted out amongst our settlement for uppards of twenty or thirty year, maybe more. I reckon folks all knows hit air bad luck to talk with the dumb show folks or guess who they air. Now then we aim to start.

(*The PRESENTER goes into the cabin and comes out walking backward with a broom.*)

PRESENTER: Out comes I hind part before,

With my big broom to sweep up the floor.

(He sweeps a wide circle, all the time muttering over and over.)

Room, room, gallons of room.

(When a circle of sufficient size has been swept, he stops muttering and begins the presentation of characters. When each character's name is called, the character struts around the outside of the circle and steps out of the circle until his part in the action of the play.)

PRESENTER: 1. In comes old Father Christmas,
Welcome or not, welcome or not,
I hope old Father Christmas
Never is forgot, never is forgot.

2. In comes old Dame Dorothy,
Drinking liquor's all her folly,
Wearing silks and being bawdy.

3. Old Bet comes in once a year
To get her kissed and bring good cheer.

4. Oh the next that now comes in
Is The Bessie as you see,
He's a woman or a man
With a cow's tail, can you see?

5. In steps black-faced
Little Devil Doubt,
Humped over bad
Toting his burdens about.

6. Pickle Herring he comes in
To join the dance,
Wearing a bedgown
Instead of his pants.

7. Here's the Doctor pure and good
With his pills he stops the blood.

(The PRESENTER *steps back among the spectators and* FATHER CHRISTMAS *and* DAME DOROTHY *enter the circle.*

OLD BET *and* THE BESSIE *tease the audience, she pretending to kiss the men, he the women.*)

FATHER CHRISTMAS: Here comes I, old Father Christmas,
      welcome or not;
      I hope old Father Christmas will
      never be forgot.
      We are come to laugh and cheer,
      And if our pudding it be done,
      We'll fry this hare and have some fun.

DAME DOROTHY: I'll beat it and bale it
      And cut it in slices,
      And take an old pot,
      And boil it with spices.

FATHER CHRISTMAS: You'll fry this hare and yet no word
      be said,
      For if you dare to boil the hare,
      With my pan I'll crack your head.

DAME DOROTHY: How can you crack my head?
      My head is made of steel.

(THE BESSIE *and* OLD BET *join the chorus and they repeat all conversation up to the time of the arrival of the Doctor.*)

DAME DOROTHY: I'll cut you into buttonholes,
      And make your buttons fly.

FATHER CHRISTMAS: I'll fill your body full of bullets,
      And make your blood fly.

DAME DOROTHY: I'll cut your coat all full of holes,
      And make the rags fly.

FATHER CHRISTMAS: I'll cut you down the middle,
      And make your blood to fly.

DAME DOROTHY: I'll cut you small as flies,
      And use you up to cook mince pies.

FATHER CHRISTMAS: If your blood is hot,
      I'll make it cold,
      As cold as muddy clay.

> I'll take your life and blood,
> And throw the hare away.

(They fight. THE BESSIE *and* OLD BET *join them.* DAME DOROTHY *is helped by* THE BESSIE, FATHER CHRISTMAS *by* OLD BET.)

DAME DOROTHY *(showing the red paper on her breast)*:
> Old Father Christmas,
> See what you've done!
> You've bloody killed
> Your own loved one! *(Falls dead.)*

*(*THE BESSIE *and* OLD BET *run away.)*

FATHER CHRISTMAS: Horrible, terrible,
> See what I've done!
> I cut her down
> Like the evening sun! *(The Chorus repeats.)*
> Is there a doctor to be found
> To cure her of this deep and deadly wound? *(Chorus)*
> Oh is there a doctor near at hand
> To heal her wound and make her stand?

(The Chorus, which has been repeating all conversations up until now, repeats the last of FATHER CHRISTMAS' *speech and is silent until the end of the play.)*

DOCTOR GOOD *(enters with* PICKLE HERRING, *who weeps over* DAME DOROTHY):
> Yes, there is a doctor near at hand
> To heal her wound and make her stand.

FATHER CHRISTMAS: What can you cure?

DOCTOR GOOD: I can cure the itch, the spots, and gout,
> If there's nine devils in, I take six out.

FATHER CHRISTMAS: What's your fee, Doctor?

DOCTOR GOOD: Fifteen pounds, it is my fee.

FATHER CHRISTMAS: Work your cure and let me see.

DOCTOR GOOD: I will. Where's Pickle Herring?

PICKLE HERRING: Oh here's Pickle Herring.

DOCTOR GOOD: Hold up her head.

PICKLE HERRING: Will she bite?

DOCTOR GOOD: Yes.

PICKLE HERRING: Will she kick?

DOCTOR GOOD: Yes.

PICKLE HERRING: Hold her yourself, then.

DOCTOR GOOD: What's that, you rascal?

PICKLE HERRING: Oh I hold her, sir.

(*He raises* DAME DOROTHY's *head.* DOCTOR GOOD *gives her a pill. She jumps up.*)

DAME DOROTHY: Once I was dead and now I'm alive.
                      Blessed be the man that made me re-
                      vive.

DEVIL DOUBT (*entering*): In comes I, Little Devil Doubt,
                      With all my family on my back.
                      Christmas comes but once a year,
                      And when it comes it brings good
                      cheer.

(DEVIL DOUBT *takes* FATHER CHRISTMAS' *pan and collects gifts of people and lays them on the* LITTLE TEACHER's *hearth each time he gets a panful. The Chorus sings "Jingle Bells" and "Come All Ye Faithful" while he is making the collection. When* DEVIL DOUBT *returns the pan,* FATHER CHRISTMAS *sweeps everybody out of the circle and then sweeps the hearth in the teacher's cabin, explaining that it is bad luck to carry out ashes on Christmas Day.*)

FATHER CHRISTMAS: Our show is done, we stay no longer
                      here.
                      God bless the mistress of this house,

> And when she wakes up Christmas
> Day,
> Lord Jesus, bring her cheer.

(The mummers depart singing the "Mummers' Carol.")

THE MUMMERS' CAROL

> There is six days all in a week,
> All for a laboring man,
> But Christmas Day is the day of our Lord,
> Both Father and Son.
> Our Christmas celebrate, my man,
> Down your knees do fall,
> And then do pray the Lord Jesus Christ
> To bless and save you all.

Seeking Jesus

Right after the war a great many Negroes came into the interior of Georgia from the sea islands of South Carolina and Georgia. They brought with them a religious festival or custom called "Seeking Jesus." They would congregate in a cabin, all the lights and fires would be put out, when one among the number would call out, "Where is Jesus?" Some one would answer: "Here is Jesus." They would rush to the part of the cabin where the answer was given, and, of course, not finding him there, would say, "He ain't here." Then another voice would cry out in the darkness from another part of the cabin: "Here is Jesus." Another rush would be made, when the statement, "He is not here," would again be made. The calls and answers would be repeated for hours, sometimes all night. The women and men would become excited and frantic, would tear their hair, and scream and pray until the meeting was broken up in a religious frenzy.

Mother, Mother, the Milk's Boiling Over

DRAMATIS PERSONAE

Mother	Hired girl
Thief	Children

MOTHER:	(*Naming* CHILDREN) Monday, Tuesday, Wednesday, Thursday, Friday, Saturday, Sunday. Goodbye, be good children! (*Exit* MOTHER)
THIEF:	Have you anything in the house?
HIRED GIRL:	Ham. (*Or anything else*)
THIEF:	Go and get some.
HIRED GIRL:	(*Aside*) Mother, mother, the milk's boiling over.
MOTHER:	(*In the distance*) Take the spoon and stir it.
HIRED GIRL:	Mother, I can't reach it.
MOTHER:	Take the chair.
HIRED GIRL:	The chair is broke.
MOTHER:	Then, I suppose I'll have to come home. (*Enters and counts the* CHILDREN.) Where's Monday at?
HIRED GIRL:	The thief's took her. (*Is beaten by the* MOTHER.)
MOTHER:	Where's Tuesday at?
HIRED GIRL:	The thief's took her. (*So the inquisition continues, until the* MOTHER *finds that all the* CHILDREN *have been taken.*)
MOTHER:	(*Approaching* THIEF) Have you seen my children?
THIEF:	I saw them go down bowlegged street.
MOTHER:	(*Walking bowlegged*) Have you seen my children?
THIEF:	They've gone down pigeon-toed street.

MOTHER: (*Walking pigeon-toed*) Have you seen any of my children?

THIEF: They've gone washing their face.

MOTHER: (*Washing her face*) Have you seen my children?

THIEF: They've gone eating bread and butter.

MOTHER: (*Making motions as though eating*) Have you any fresh chickens?

THIEF: I'll have them done tomorrow at one o'clock.

MOTHER: (*After interval*) Have you any fresh chickens?

THIEF: I'll have them done tomorrow at two o'clock. (*So the* THIEF *keeps putting off the* MOTHER *until the promise is for "tomorrow at twelve o'clock."*)

MOTHER: Lemme go in and see them.

THIEF: Your shoes are too dirty.

MOTHER: I'll take them off.

THIEF: Your stockings are too dirty.

MOTHER: I'll take them off.

THIEF: Your feet are too big.

MOTHER: I'll take them off.

THIEF: Your feet are too bloody.

(*At this, the children all run out from their hiding place.*)

A Ring Game from North Carolina

GRANDDADDY IS DEAD

One player lies stretched on the ground for granddaddy; another represents the tree, waves his hands for apples falling; another player outside of the ring represents the old lady. "Granddaddy" jumps up and thumps her. The player who represents the old woman, the next time represents the old man.

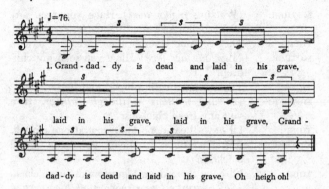

1. Grand-dad-dy is dead and laid in his grave, laid in his grave, laid in his grave, Grand-dad-dy is dead and laid in his grave, Oh heigh oh!

2. There grew an old apple-tree
   Over his head,
   Over his head,
   Over his head,
   Oh heigh oh!

3. The apples got ripe and began to fall:
   Then came an old woman
   A-pickin' them up,
   A-pickin' them up,
   A-pickin' them up.

4. Granddaddy jumped up
   And gave her a thump,
   Gave her a thump,
   Gave her a thump,
   Oh heigh oh!

A Slovak Harvest Festival in New Jersey

Plans were being made for the harvest celebration. "There will be two rented trucks. People in costumes will be peasants, and go in the second truck; the others will dress as farmers and go on the first. You know, it is a small

town and people are sensitive . . . America first. I will
dress as a farmer and perhaps take the big hat of an American farmer. The peasants will go behind as if they were
only accompanying the farmers to the dance. The sheaves
and wreaths will be bought from a dealer in Trenton—here
they cut the grain differently, only the ears, and leave the
straw standing in the fields. We will start at the other end
of town as if there were fields. We will go slowly through
the town as if it were a village, to the clubhouse, as if it
were a farm. There the Porubskýs will await us with drinks
and food. They will be the landowners; they are the oldest
among us and they are here thirty years already. Someone
should write about it in the newspapers so that the other
people would know what it is. It is not easy to go through
the whole town. They might throw tomatoes at us. Or
perhaps the Ukrainians and Poles will think that it is something political. . . ." Anna Nekarda joined in at this point:
"No one can harm us. No one can do anything to us. We
are supposed to . . . we signed to do it . . . to cultivate
the old customs." Later she told me, "I will not go on the
truck. I don't feel like it. It is not sincere. I don't feel like
one of them. It is an imitation, do you know what I mean?"

The next day we were standing on the outskirts of
Heightstown [New Jersey] waiting. In each truck there
were about forty people with scythes, rakes, and forks in
their hands. There were also sheaves, wreaths, samples of
grain, ribbons, green twigs and accordions. The peasants
and farmers were discussing what songs to sing when they
went through the center of town. Should it be the American "Old MacDonald had a farm, quack, quack, quack?
. . . then there should be ducks and pigs on the truck
also, but the ducks are not harvested . . ." The hour
struck and the procession moved on. I was asked to join
the young people in the first car behind the trucks. The
young president of the entertainment branch of the club,
who was supposed to organize the celebration together
with the parents, was driving. As soon as we started, the

boys hurriedly pulled down the curtains, huddled together, choked with laughter and embarrassment: "The people in town know us and we don't want them to see us here." "How could my mother ever go on the truck, and so madly dressed?" The young president was pale and tight-lipped. "I didn't want it this way at all . . . it slipped out of my hands," he said to me almost apologetically. The songs grew louder as we neared the town. I opened the window. The ribbons flew, the songs became solemn, and I saw Jožka [Nekarda] in front, waving his hat in the air. His voice was leading. However, there was no one in the streets. It was a hot Sunday noon in Indian Summer. The people didn't open their windows to look, nor did the few pedestrians turn or wave. We were already in the Negro quarter and there they looked at us lazily without even a smile. From the town on, we went faster and faster through the fields to the forest. At the club someone took pictures of the "peasants" and the "farmers" with their sheaves, wreaths, and tools. Then we went inside where the "landowners" were waiting. An old ritual song was sung to wish them well, while some were helping me to place my recording machine so that they would all be heard on it. They were delighted. The Porubskýs served drinks and a cake, and we danced until morning. . . .

Three years ago at Easter time, [Sam] Černek came to visit a Slovak family in Manhattan, and there I met him for the first time. With a willow whip he was to perform the traditional whipping of the women and to get painted eggs from them in return. Every year he makes this visit to his numerous friends in New York and vicinity. "There wouldn't be any Easter without it." Later, however, he told me, referring to the ceremonial whipping, "It is nothing. It is in name only. It is to commemorate that in our country we used to whip the Christ. It is not real. You should have seen our theater. We played the Harvest. It was called *The Peasant from the Golden Farm*, and there was everything. It was exactly like at home. I was the landowner. God, it was beautiful!"

The play was performed again the following fall. The dramatis personae in the production included the landowner, his wife and nephew; a poor peasant and his daughter; the priest, mayor, and innkeeper; the night watchman and the policeman; the matchmaker; a maid; first, second, and third neighbors; farmhands, maidservants, and musicians. The orchestra was to play during and after the performance. The curtain rose, and on the stage there was a Slovak village: a peasant house at the left with a high gable and a red geranium in a small window; a tree was at the right, and in the background were mountains covered with forests and a light blue sky. A cock crowed; it was morning. It was just like home, and beautiful, I thought. The plot developed rapidly, and the second act started with the harvest celebration. The stage was crowded with peasants and their children. The reapers came from the fields with a sheaf and a wreath, with wreaths on their heads and tools in their hands. They sang the ritual song for the landowner and his wife, who stood in front of their house, ate the ritual cake, and drank the liquor which was offered to them. They danced around the sheaf and the landowner couple and sang many harvesting songs. The impression of gaiety was successfully produced and the scene was applauded. The landowner was exuberant; his improvised jokes were especially rewarded with outbursts of laughter from the audience.

A Corpus Christi Festival in Pennsylvania

Christmas and Easter are duly observed, but the great day of the year is the Festival of Corpus Christi, in honor of Christ's triumphant entry into Jerusalem, and the institution of the Sacrament of the Lord's Supper which followed. The festival was observed this year on Sunday,

June 19, with great pomp and ceremony, and we were so fortunate as to see it. Preparations for it began in St. Mary's and the outlying farms a week before. The large and beautiful German Catholic Church, where the procession was to form, was decorated with evergreens and flowers more profusely than at Christmas or Easter. On the Saturday before, the farmers brought green saplings and boughs from the woods and stuck them in the earth along the route of the procession. Baskets of cut flowers, green leaves, fresh ferns, and grasses were provided for strewing in the road before the Host, and in all German homes great preparations were made for the feast which was to follow at the close of the ceremonies, the day having as great significance in this respect as Thanksgiving in New England. The route of the procession was to be from the German church to the pretty hilltop cemetery a half mile distant, and return by another road. At intervals along the way, wayside altars were erected—bowers of greenery bedecked with flowers and bearing a Christ on the cross, pictures of the Virgin and saints, and other emblems of the Catholic faith. Lighted candles burned before these shrines during the ceremonies.

The day began with the celebration of Low Mass at eight o'clock. Long before this, the streets were filled with happy groups wending their way toward the church, all attired in gala dress—girls in white, with long white veils floating behind, and bearing bouquets of flowers in their hands; boys each with a boutonniere in his coat lapel; mothers with babes in arms, and fathers escorting them. Great farm wagons, drawn by horses or mules, came lumbering in from the farms, their seats filled with farmer folk having the rugged German features, clad in the garb of the German peasant, and addressing one another in the language of the fatherland.

When the celebration of High Mass began, at nine o'clock, the church was crowded to suffocation, and the worshipers filled the portico and esplanade. At ten, at the conclusion of the service, the procession was formed, the Father Prior acting as master of ceremonies. First came three acolytes in altar vestments, bearing emblems of the Catholic faith; then a standard-bearer with the banner of the Holy Childhood Society of the parish. The members of the society followed—the boys first, and then the girls, the latter, some five hundred in number, clad in white dresses and veils, and bearing baskets of flowers, which they strewed along the road; after them the St. Mary's Silver Cornet Band, then one each of the men's and women's societies of the parish, bearing banners; after them, under a rich canopy borne by four men, came three Benedictine fathers in full canonicals, the central one, a monk of imposing presence, bearing the Sacred Host. Next came more parish societies of both sexes bearing banners; then the St. Mary's Citizen Band; then devotees in general, the whole procession numbering fully two thousand persons, and stretching from the church to the cemetery. As the head of the procession approached the first of the wayside altars, the boys uncovered their heads, and all chanted hymns in praise of the Christ and of the Sacrament. As the priests with the Sacred Host arrived before the altar, the procession halted, and the priests, kneeling before it, performed the appropriate service for Corpus Christi, and bestowed the Benedictus, the whole body of people kneeling during the ceremony. The procession then continued on to the German cemetery, with its quaint Old World tombs and crosses, past the little chapel in its midst, where prayers and masses for the dead are said, and out by another entrance. As the priests arrived at the door of the chapel the people again halted, the celebrants entered and performed the same service as at the altar. The march was again resumed, and the procession returned to the church by another road, passing a second wayside altar, before which the solemn service was again performed. At the church, the procession was disbanded, the members returning to their homes to enjoy the feast which had been prepared for the occasion, perhaps to meet long-sundered members of the family around the board.

The *Penitentes* of New Mexico

The Holy Week ceremonies begin on Wednesday or Thursday, with religious meetings during the day and a procession with the *carreta de la muerte*. This cart of death is drawn by a man or men by their necks or other parts of their bodies so as to make this penitential task extremely difficult. Sometimes a man pulls the cart by what seems a good, broad leather belt around his chest— but there is cactus under the belt! Tradition says that during this procession the effigy of death may loose her arrow at the unbelieving scoffer. The *carretas* seen by the author ranged from two to three feet in height and from two to four feet in length, all with solid wooden wheels. At this and other processions the hand-carved *santos* [saints] of the local area are often carried. In this particular religious procession, the priest is conspicuous by his absence. The *Cristo* [Christ] has been chosen, by lot or election, within the *morada* [meetinghouse of the sect]. No extreme honor is attached to enacting *Cristo*, but the person is usually below middle age, a devout *Penitente*, and is not chosen twice.

Within one or two hundred yards of the *morada* there is a hill known as *Calvario* [Calvary]. Late Holy Thursday night a formal procession of true flagellation occurs. At the head of the procession usually comes a statue of Christ, or some *santos*. Next comes the chosen *Cristo* dragging his cross on his right shoulder. He is aided by an *acompañador* [accompanying brother] who represents Simon of Cyrene. Often others, representing the two thieves, also carry crosses, but the number depends on the size of the local lodge. All the members are present, the *pitero* playing his flute, and the *rezador* praying or reading from his hand-written copybook. All chant *alabados,* more or less in unison, which urge penance and plead for salvation and mercy. Those actually engaged in flagellation march in the center of the procession, surrounded by *acompaña-dores* or *compañeros* who carry lanterns, help those who fall, lend both moral and physical support to the ceremony, and throw rocks at non-members who have failed to remain at a respectful distance. In general the officers of a local chapter are called *Hermanos de la Luz.* This is usually translated Brothers of Light, which term is sometimes used when speaking of the whole cult. The Brothers of Light usually are those who have flagellated themselves in earlier years. The common members are called Brothers of Darkness, possibly because during flagellation they are supposed to wear hoods. When one ceases his flagellation and in the next procession acts as an *acompañador,* he is said to have "returned to light." These references to "light" and "darkness," so reminiscent of the ancient influence of Zoroastrianism on Judaism, have long since lost any such esoteric meaning for the *Penitentes.*

Those actually engaged in flagellation who wear black hoods over their heads do so partly to keep their identity secret, partly to prevent pride. Their backs are bare, they may wear a crown of thorns, and their trousers may be the traditional white *pantalones* of the *peón;* their feet are bare. The whips used are of various types; often they are of the type of yucca cactus locally called *amole* or Spanish dagger. These whips are about three feet long, four inches wide, and an inch thick, with the fibers pounded out to resemble a frayed rope, if one can imagine a rope with ravelings which cut like sandpaper with each slanting blow. Other whips have leather thongs and leather or wooden handles. Rarely are the leather thongs plain; at the least they contain knots, at the worst they hold bits of glass, lead balls, or the barbs taken from barbed wire.

When the *Penitentes* chant of "giving their blood," this is no idly symbolic term.

Usually one or more of the *Penitentes*, instead of scourging himself, will walk in the processions with cactus bound tightly to his bare back and chest, dragging heavy chains from raw ankles. Various thorns and cactus can be used, for the stark, brutal flora of the area offer adequate variety for anyone's satisfaction. Those *Penitentes* actively flagellating themselves usually take a few steps, swing the *disciplina* [whip] over one shoulder, take a few more steps, and swing it over the other shoulder, pausing with each blow. Before a hundred yards is passed, the whip has little fresh skin to touch, blood spatters at every stroke, and may so stain the trousers that the legs, too, appear to bleed. It is no wonder a *Penitente* flagellant march sometimes is called the "Procession of Blood." In older days unbleached trousers were worn; today they are likely to be faded blue jeans. Often a white handkerchief is tied around the forehead of all the members as a sort of recognition sign. The wounds, although exceedingly painful, are not deep and the muscle structure is not damaged. After a few months, remarkably little scarring remains. Although cactus may be stuck to any portion of the body, flagellation is confined solely to the back and shoulders.

During the night a *velorio* [vigil] usually is kept by non-members of the society at the local church. This *velorio* is visited sometime during the night by a procession from the *morada*. *Alabados* are sung by the persons keeping the vigil. These *alabados*, like many of the rituals, are in a Spanish pronunciation no longer in normal use, with many ancient words and forms of speech preserved nowhere else. Typically one or two good singers carry the solo parts with the rest of the men singing the chorus. Women do not participate fully in the singing of *alabados* and in general they are sung chiefly by members of the brotherhood.

On Good Friday further ceremonies and processions occur. As in the previous processions, the line of march varies from village to village but, sooner or later, processions, complete with banners, *santos,* flagellation, and men dragging crosses, will visit the cemetery and the chapel or church, and then return to the *morada.* The chief Good Friday procession, usually in the afternoon, is the march to Calvary. Before undertaking this final act of penance a rather lengthy service is held in the *morada* chapel, with chants, prayers, and hymns. After night has fallen comes the final and most barbaric of all the processions. This is the enactment of the crucifixion, with the thorn-crowned *Cristo* again staggering under his cross to *Calvario* and with brutal scourging of already lacerated backs. When *Calvario* is reached, the cross is placed in a previously prepared hole with the *Cristo* upon it. In the old days a hammer drove iron nails through his hands and feet; more recently the *Cristo* is tied with thongs. In either case, at this point all those in the procession as well as the families and friends, kneel and pray, say rosaries and chant. Often a brief sermon is given by a *Penitente.* Usually the *Cristo* has fainted before even this brief service is over; the cross with the man still on it is taken down and borne quickly and triumphantly back to the *morada.* The *alabados* chanted on the return procession are triumphant, and there is no whipping. In the *morada* the erstwhile Christ is cared for. In the old days the *Cristo's* side was slashed, and occasionally he died. It is said that in such a case the man was immediately buried and his shoes placed outside the door of his house to signify his passing. There are constantly recurring rumors of the recent re-use of nails, side slashing, and deaths, but the extreme secrecy of the order makes this impossible for a non-member to trace to a specific village in a specific year.

A Lenten Procession in Arizona

As my parents and I waited beside the dusty, moonlit plaza, the descending minor call of a Yaqui flute floated across to us, and shortly thereafter the sound of a church bell. Then we heard the rhythmic tapping of the Chapaye-kas' wooden daggers against their wooden swords, and we knew the procession had started. First came two Chapaye-kas escorting Pilate, head of the Fariseo society, next came men carrying a huge gray cross and stalked by half a dozen leering Chapayekas. [These clown-like figures, carrying painted wooden swords and wearing painted hide headmasks, blankets, and chains of deerhide rattles, per-sonify the enemies of Christ.] Then we saw the girl and boy angels and the maestro, or prayer reader, accompa-nied by men carrying gasoline lanterns, and finally a little group of women carrying three sacred images of the Virgin Mary. As they marched, the women chanted hymns which made a strange counterpoint to the staccato rhythm of the drum, flute, and wooden swords.

The procession soon passed from our view at the east entrance of the churchyard in its slow counterclockwise march around the plaza. Although we could not see it, we could hear the beating sticks and rattling belts as the clownish Chapayekas pantomimed their resentment of the worshiping faithful. It took a long time—almost an hour— for the procession to reach our position at the sixth station of the cross. We saw the Chapayekas coming first. They seemed to be looking for footprints in the dust. Then came the men carrying the heavy gray cross. They stopped on the far side of the yellow mesquite cross marking the sta-tion and turned to face the rest of the oncoming proces-sion. At the opposite side of the station the boy angels drew up in a line, with the women singers, girl angels, and congregation back of them. Between the two facing groups

the maestro sank to his knees, and by the light of a gasoline lantern began to read in Spanish the appropriate
prayers for that station. At last he finished, the Chapayekas
shook themselves and beat their swords, the flute and
drum sounded, and the procession resumed its way. . . .

Many of the changes in the Yaqui penitential processions appear to be the result of the mixing of Indian and
Spanish cultural elements. Thus, the hide headmask of
the Chapayekas seems to have been introduced both as a
dramatic prop and as a substitute for the Spanish *capirote*
[conical hood]. Yet, in its traditional form, it seems to be
derived from pre-Conquest headmasks of the Yaquis and
other Southwestern Indian groups. Similarly, the Yaqui
flute and drum have aboriginal as well as European pro-
totypes. . . .

The sharp contrast in the Yaqui Friday processions between the pantomimed blasphemies of the unbaptized
Chapayekas and the pure devotion of the child angels,
maestros, singers, and altar women clearly illustrates the
procession's dramatic function. This function, in turn, may
be traced to the Church's use of the drama as a means of
indoctrination. Yaqui vestiges of the religious folk drama of
Los Pastores and of the dance drama of *Moors and Chris-
tians* offer further evidence that such media helped to give
the Yaqui penitential processions their dramatic and mil-
itary character.

NOTES ON SOURCES

ABBREVIATIONS USED IN NOTES

A-T   Antti Aarne and Stith Thompson, *The Types of the Folktale* (rev. ed.). Helsinki: 1961.

Boggs   Ralph S. Boggs, *Index of Spanish Tales*. Helsinki: Folklore Fellows Communications No. 90, 1930.

Brown   Newman Ivy White, *The Frank C. Brown Collection of North Carolina Folklore*. 6 vol. Durham: Duke University Press, 1952–64.

Child   Francis James Child, *The English and Scottish Popular Ballads*. 5 vol. Boston: 1882–98.

Coffin   Tristram P. Coffin, *The British Traditional Ballad in North America* (Bibliographical and Special Series, II [rev. ed.]). Philadelphia: American Folklore Society, 1963.

Dorson   Richard M. Dorson, *Negro Folktales in Michigan*. Cambridge: Harvard University Press, 1956.

JAF   *Journal of American Folklore*. Philadelphia: American Folklore Society, 1888 to the present.

Laws, *ABBB*   G. Malcolm Laws, Jr., *American Balladry from British Broadsides* (Bibliographical and Special Series, VIII). Philadelphia: American Folklore Society, 1957.

Laws, *NAB*   G. Malcolm Laws, Jr., *Native American Balladry* (Bibliographical and Special Series, I [rev. ed.]). Philadelphia: American Folklore Society, 1964.

Motif   Stith Thompson, *Motif-Index of Folk Literature*. 6 vols. Bloomington: Indiana University Press, 1955.

The Folktale

Turtle Surpasses Man in Ingenuity, 1914, 271.
  African Bulu, evidently from Kamerum, West Africa. Collected by George Schwab. Date, exact place, and informant not given. See Motif H 1023.2. This tale has been included because it is characteristic of the stories the slaves brought with them to America.

Saru-to-kani, 1946, 291–92.
  Japanese. Collected by Miss N. I. in 1934 in either Berkeley or Oakland. Informant and translator not given. This is a well-known Japanese tale. See Motifs K 1600 f. and J 1510 f.

Adam and Eve and Their Children, 1936, 119.
  American Indian. Collected by Aurelio M. Espinosa in 1931 from the Isleta Pueblo Indians. Exact date and informant not given. See Motif A 1650.1.

The Bear Husband, 1944, 162–63.
  Armenian. Collected in Detroit by Susie Hoogasian and edited by Emelyn E. Gardner, from Mrs. Mary Srabian, born in Harpoot, Armenia, arrived in America in 1924, as told in 1940. Recorded in shorthand and later translated into English. See the note in *JAF* (1944), 163. A-T 301 (I).

Min Tzŭ Chien, 1923, 30.
  Manchurian. Written down for Edward Sapir by Hsü Tsan Hwa, Secretary of the Chinese Consulate in Canada. Date and place not given. The tale is one of the twenty-four famous Chinese tales of filial piety. See Motifs L 50 and S 31.

Les Cartes du Nommé Richard, 1916, 134.
  French Canadian. Collected in Lorette, Quebec, by C.-Marius Barbeau in August 1914 from P. Sioui, as learned from his father Clément Sioui. Translated by T.P.C., Motif H 603. The informant forgot the symbolism of the nine: "The nine ungrateful lepers." A more common symbolism for the ace is "one God, one Faith, one Baptism."

The Priestwife Gets a Beating, 1947, 167.
  Greek. Collected by Dorothy D. Lee in Boston between 1934 and 1937. Informant not given. See A-T 882 and 1419H for stories that are quite similar.

The King and Old George Buchanan, 1925, 370–71.
  Scottish. Collected by Isabel Gordon Carter from Susie Wil-

kinson of Elkmont, Tennessee, in the summer of 1923. Buchanan, the tutor of James VI, developed into a legendary figure. See J. F. Campbell, *Popular Tales of the West Highlands* (London, 1890–93), II, 406; A-T 921; and Motifs H 561.5, H 583.3, H 583.5, H 1054.3 f., and J 1189.

Dividing the Chicken, 1918, 555.
Irish. Collected by Archer Taylor from C. N. Gould who got it in southern Minnesota about 1885 from Julian Christensen (from Laaland, Denmark) who had learned it from an Irishman in North Dakota. See Taylor's note in *JAF* (1918), 555–56 for a history of the tale. Also see A-T 1533.

An Alsatian Witch Story, 1906, 242.
German from Canada. Collected by W. J. Wintemberg. Date, exact place, informant not given. A variant of this story appears in Leonard W. Roberts, *South from Hell-fer-sartin*, Publications of the Council of the Southern Mountains (Berea, Ky., 1964), 108, No. 35 b. See Motifs G 224.2, G 241.1.6, G 242.1.1, and G 242.7, as well as D 1531.7.

Why the Irish Came to America, 1933, 90–91.
Irish-American. Collected by Charles Neely in the area of southern Illinois known as Egypt from Frank Schumaker of Grand Tower. Date not given. A-T 465 and 330 B.

Brer Rabbit's Cool Air Swing, 1900, 22–23.
American Negro. Collected by Emma M. Backus in Georgia. Date, exact place, informant not given. Motifs K 621 and K 842.1.

Valpariso and Lily White, 1934, 377–78.
Dutch-American. Collected by Henrietta Corson Harris as "told by Grandma Harriett Corson Harris to her children and grandchildren." "By a Dutch girl," place, date, and exact informant not given. See A-T 313 A and motifs listed there.

The Flute Player, 1925, 303–4.
Micmac-Negro Half Breed. Collected in Lequille, Nova Scotia, by Arthur H. Fauset from Joe Pennall in 1923. This story is most likely Irish in origin and of the Motif F 262 group. See also Motifs G 303, K 10–100, and M 210; as well as A-T 1060–1114. In some ways it is reminiscent of the flute contests involving Apollo.

The Mean Rich Man, 1935, 177.
Spanish-American. Collected by Helen Zunser in Hot Springs, New Mexico, from Antonio Lorenz. Date and translator not given. A-T 1561.

Wait Till Emmett Comes, 1934, 352–54.
   American Negro. Collected by John Harrington Cox from Miss
A. Lulu Hill in East St. Louis in October 1925. See Cox's note
in *JAF* (1934), 352; and Dorson, Footnote 85. Motif
J 1495.2.

The Man Who Plucked the Corberie, 1961, 5.
   Anglo-American. Collected by Edward D. Ives by mail from
A. Richard of Brunswick, Maine, "as it was told us when we
were kids by my grandfather as a bedtime story." Date not
given. See Ives' notes in *JAF* (1961), 7–8. A *corberie* (*cor-
bie*) or *gorby* is Scottish for crow or raven. Here it is used
for the Canada Jay.

Big Lies from Grassy, 1934, 390–91.
   Anglo-American. Collected by June Clark from "the driver of
a mule team during a drive with him in Elliot County, Kentucky." Date not given. See Motifs X 1130.2 f., X 1132.1,
and F 54.2.

A Numskull Story, 1941, 56–57.
   Anglo-American. Collected by Grace Partridge Smith from
Wendell Margrave in Thebes, Illinois, in the southern area
popularly known as Egypt "after a tale heard from a lawyer
in Jonesboro." Date not given. See the note in *JAF* (1941),
56–57; and Motifs J 1730 f., J 1930 f., and X 1761.

The Preacher and the Hog, 1934, 380.
   Anglo-American. Collected by Thomas B. Stroup in Septem-
ber 1931 in Fletcher, North Carolina, from a member of "the
mountain branch of my own family." A similar tale about a
sheep is the central event in *The Second Shepherd's Play*
written in the mid-fifteenth century by the so-called Wake-
field Master. A-T 1525 M.

Rip Van Winkle, 1945, 217–18.
   Spanish-American. Collected by Calvin Claudel as written by
Katherine Sartalamacchia in 1941 at Violet, St. Bernard Par-
ish, Louisiana. See the famous story by Washington Irving
and the note in *JAF* (1945), 218. Also see A-T 766; and
Motif D 1960.1.

Juan José, 1929, 136.
   Puerto Rican. Collected by J. Alden Mason in Puerto Rico in
1914–15, edited by Aurelio M. Espinosa, translated by T.P.C.
Exact place, informant not given. See Dorson, Footnote 47;
and A-T 1700. Motif J 2496.2.

The Fire-Hunt, 1934, 270.

Anglo-American. Printed by Ralph S. Boggs from Harden E. Taliaferro's *Fisher's River (N.C.) Scenes and Characters* (New York, 1859), 154. The tale was undoubtedly known to Taliaferro from oral tradition and in this variant probably dates from about 1820. A "quiz" is a prankster. The torch and pan are used in the same way a modern hunter might use a flashlight or headlights to help him shoot game. O'Pan is Uncle Billy's favorite gun. See Boggs' notes in *JAF* (1934), 270, 318. Motif F 491.1.

Shakespeare's Ghost, 1956, 74–75.

Anglo-American. Collected by Herbert Halpert from Charles H. Grant in New Egypt, New Jersey, the ballad on August 14, 1938, and the story on July 30, 1939. See the note in *JAF* (1956), 75, 98. The ballad is Child No. 78; see Coffin, 77. The tale resembles the story of Héloïse and Abélard; see Motif Q 451.10.

Stories about Mr. Mac, 1950, 467–68.

Anglo-American. Collected by Kenneth W. Porter as "they were attached to a family in my own midwestern home town." Date, informant, exact place not given. See Motifs W 152 f.

How the Town Was Named Elkader, 1949, 318.

Anglo-American. Collected by Helen Rosemary Cole from the Elkader Hills (Little Switzerland), Iowa. Date, informant not given. This tale, obviously restyled by the collector, is typical of the sentimental, semi-literary local legends which are known to every community in America.

Night Doctors, 1928, 546.

Negro. Collected in Philadelphia by Arthur H. Fauset in early 1923. No. 1 is from James Perrin, who was born in North Carolina, and in 1923 was a barber in New York and Philadelphia. No. 2 is from a Mr. Parker, who was raised in North Carolina. A night doctor procures bodies for sale to medical researchers by any means. See Motifs G 440 and R 11.

The Soldier Who Used His Head, 1949, 176.

U. S. Army. Collected by Norris Yates from Pvt. William H. Beverley en route to Camp Stoneman, California. Date not given. This is an old hunting tale, often attached to the Jim Bridger legends. A-T 1890 E.

The Three Chaplains Play Cards, 1964, 336.

Jewish. Collected by Ed Cray in Los Angeles in August 1960

from an actor, Herschel Bernardi. See the comment following
the story in *JAF* (1964), 336. Also see A-T 1839.

Using the Telephone, 1948, 141.
  Cornish-American. Collected by Richard M. Dorson on May
  15, 1946, from Walter F. Gries in Ishpeming, Michigan. This
  is an old vaudeville joke.

THE FOLKSONG

The Two Sisters, 1932, 7–8.
  Anglo-American. Recorded by Mrs. Mellinger Henry from
  Mrs. Samuel Harmon of Cade's Cove, Blount County, Tennessee, on August 13, 1930. This is a variant of Child No. 10.
  For a full bibliography and discussion see Coffin, 32–36,
  where the present text is printed as Story Type C. The plot is
  from an old and widely known folktale: see A-T 780.

An Indian Love Song, 1888, 210–11.
  American Indian. Dictated to J. Owen Dorsey by Francis
  La Flèche, then of the Indian Bureau. The song is from the
  Omaha Sioux. Date, place, and informant not given. The
  translation is that originally printed by Dorsey in *JAF*.

La Randonnée de la Ville de Paris, 1919, 68–69.
  French Canadian. Collected by E.-Z. Massicotte in Montreal
  from Alfred Legault who learned it in 1906 in Montreal from
  Joseph Larin who learned it from his father from Cédres.
  Prepared by C.-Marius Barbeau; translated by T.P.C. See *JAF*
  (1919), 68, Footnote 1. The song is widely known in Europe
  and America. Usually, there is a bird in the egg, a wing on
  the bird, a feather on the wing, etc.

Trippa, Troppa, Tronjes, 1953, 60.
  Dutch-American. Recorded by Constance V. Ring from Mrs.
  Grispell Broadhead of Old Hurley, New York, in July 1925.
  See the note in *JAF* (1953), 59–60, where Theodore Roose-
  velt's use of it in *African Trails* (New York, 1910), 51, is
  cited. The translation is the one that appears in the Ring
  Manuscript at Vassar College.

Songs for Christmas and the New Year, 1921, 106–9.
  Cape Verde Negro. Collected by Elsie Clews Parsons from
  Portuguese Negroes in Rhode Island or Massachusetts. Date,
  exact place, informants not given. Transcribed by Helen H.
  Roberts.

The Ocean Burial, 1912, 278.
  Anglo-American. Collected by Phillips Barry from O.F.A.C. of Harrisburg, Pennsylvania. Date not given. This song is better known in its Western adaptation, "O Bury Me Not on the Lone Prairie." See *JAF* (1912), 278, Footnote 2. Also see Laws, *NAB*, 79–82, for a discussion of the present text and the Western version.

La Estrella del Norte, 1911, 323.
  Spanish-American. Collected by Eleanor Hague in Los Angeles in the spring of 1911 from Carlotta Manuela Corella, who had learned it in Mexico. The translation is the one used by the collector when she printed the song in *Spanish-American Folk Songs*, Publications of the American Folklore Society, Memoir xx (Philadelphia, 1917), 58.

Ein Stevleik, 1938, 73–75.
  Norwegian. Collected and translated by Einar Haugen. His explanatory notes from *JAF* (1938), 72–75, are reproduced with the verse.

Ten Thousand Miles Away, 1914, 75–76.
  Anglo-American. Printed by Phillips Barry from a melody and text from H.L.W. of Cambridge, Massachusetts. The text was from a manuscript owned by M.A.S. of Sidney, Kansas. According to Stan Hugill, *Shanties from the Seven Seas* (London and New York, 1961), 408, this shanty was "originally a shore ballad and later a forebitter, but which was used at times as a capstan song." See Hugill, 408–10, for a variant, other comments, and references. The parody, "The Walloping Window-Blind," had great popularity in songsters and college songbooks a couple of generations ago.

Pig in the Parlor, 1920, 117–18.
  Anglo-American. Collected by Emelyn E. Gardner from Livia Youngquist of Whitehall, Michigan, a student at Michigan State Normal College in 1914 or 1915. This is a well-known play-party and square dance song. See *JAF* (1920), 117, Footnote 1; and Brown, I, 107, for parallel texts.

I've a Long Time Heard, 1913, 153.
  Anglo-American. Collected by E. C. Perrow in Mississippi from the manuscript of J. E. Rankin, a student at the University of Mississippi in 1908. This white spiritual can be found in the Georgia *Sacred Harp* (ca. 1859), 386, "as sung by Judge Falkerner of Alabama." See also George P. Jackson, *White and Negro Spirituals* (New York, 1943), 152, No. 10.

Ain't Gwine Grieve My God No More, 1913, 374–76.
   American Negro. This spiritual was collected by Emma M.
   Backus in Grovetown, Georgia. Exact date, informant not
   given. See Howard W. Odum's notes in *JAF* (1913), 374–76,
   particularly Footnote 1 which lists parallel texts often given
   under the title "Hypocrite, Hypocrite."

Railroad Blues, 1915, 293.
   American Negro. Collected by Walter Prescott Webb near
   Beeville, Texas, from Floyd Canada. No date given. See
   Webb's note in *JAF* (1915), 291–92. Much of this song is
   made up of stanzas that "float through" southern Negro
   songs. Webb quotes his informant as saying "it is sung to the
   tune of 'The Dallas Blues.' " "The monkey motion" refers to
   the train's whistle, a "monkey" being a mechanical device.

Lob-Gesang, 1939, 92–93.
   Amish. Collected by John Umble with notation prepared by
   John Friesen of Goshen, Indiana. The background of this
   hymn, included with the text, is reproduced from the original
   printing in *JAF*. The translation is by Don Yoder.

The Death of the Beckwith Child, 1899, 242–44.
   Anglo-American. Collected by William Wells Newell from a
   manuscript owned by "a friend." Date and source not given.
   This is an excellent example of the narrative obituary verse
   often sung or distributed at funerals. Some of these pieces
   have become widely-known ballads. For an essay on the subject, see *Folksong and Folksong Scholarship* (Dallas, 1964),
   3–11.

Asesinato de Francisco Villa, 1923, 188.
   Spanish-American. From a Mexican-American broadside
   printed in Brownsville, Texas, in the summer of 1923. Sent
   to J. Frank Dobie by Julian Ashheim of Brownsville. This is
   typical of the songs that came from printing presses all over
   Europe and America during the years from 1500 to 1900.
   Many such songs became popular with the folk. Francisco
   "Pancho" Villa, born Doreteo Arango, ca. 1872–1923, was
   the Mexican general and revolutionary whose attack on Co-
   lumbus, New Mexico, in March 1916 led to U.S. intervention
   in Mexico. The broadside was translated by Américo Paredes.

Silver Jack, 1915, 9–10.
   Anglo-American. Sent to John Lomax before 1913 by Professor Edwin F. Gay of Harvard University who "says that he
   got it from a lumber camp in northern Michigan." Silver Jack
   is reportedly the notorious fighter and badman, Jack Driscoll,

who died in 1895. See Laws, *NAB*, 158–59, for bibliography, notes, and discussion.

I'm a Good Old Rebel, 1926, 172.
Anglo-American. Collected by Arthur P. Hudson from A. H. Burnette, then a student at the University of Mississippi, who learned it from his mother, Mrs. G. A. Burnette of Rena Lara, Mississippi. This song was originally a poem by Major Innes Randolph of General J. E. B. Stuart's staff. It was quite popular with die-hard Confederates during Reconstruction. See J. Harrington Cox's *Folk Songs of the South* (Cambridge, Mass., 1925), No. 77.

Bishop Zack, 1945, 293.
Mormon. Printed by Levette J. Davidson from George F. Briegel, *Old Time Mormon and Far West Songs* (New York, 1933), 38–39. See *JAF* (1945), 286. Footnote 28. This is a rewriting of "Casey Jones." See Laws, *NAB*, 212–13, G 1, for a discussion of "Casey Jones." The "D'n R. G." was the Denver and Rio Grande Railroad.

Sellin' That Stuff, 1939, 105.
Negro. Collected by Muriel Davis Longini from Negroes in Chicago. Date and informant not given. Typical of the city songs produced by the recording industry for the northern Negro ghettoes, this piece was written by Thomas A. Dorsey (Georgia Tom) and recorded on Paramount 12714 in December 1928 by The Hokum Boys. The present text is essentially that of the recording.

McKinley and Huey Long, 1950, 276–77.
Anglo-American. Collected by MacEdward Leach and Horace P. Beck from Silas Pendleton of Huntly, Virginia, in the spring of 1947. The songs, which demonstrate the way in which material is re-used as times change, contain borrowings from "Frankie and Johnny" (Laws I 3). See Laws, *NAB*, 247–48.

The Haunted Wood, 1954, 250.
Pseudo-Indian. Collected by Austin Fife and Francesca Redden from Buck Lee of Clearfield, Utah, on August 25, 1946. Transcribed by Cora Burt Lauridsen. See *JAF* (1954), 250, Footnote 83 for sources.

Rhymes from Hawaii, 1957, 215–17.
Hawaiian-American. Collected by Linton C. Freeman, whose comments and references are included with the texts.

The Dehorn Song, 1960, 198.
Anglo-American. Printed by Archie Green from the collection

of John Neuhaus as learned from "Louis Gracey, a West Coast shovel stiff and fellow worker, who taught it to him in an Oakland, California, I.W.W. Hall in 1947." See Green's remarks in *JAF* (1960), 197–98 and 206. "Dehorn" means anything in opposition to I.W.W. teachings. If one has no horns, no social consciousness, he has no weapon to fight capitalism. "Fix the job" means to sabotage the work actively or passively. "Stakebound" indicates the dehorn has made or is making a stake or amount of money on which he can live for a few days. "Sticky muck" probably refers to wet soil or some other material hard to work with, though it possibly refers to the muck stick or shovel.

SUPERSTITIONS

To Charm Cattle and Cure Injuries, 1934, 382.
Finnish. Collected by Marjorie Edgar from "settlers from Finland and their descendants" in "the iron mining towns of Minnesota and the lake country surrounding them." Charms were originally used by professional *loihtija* or wise women. Names of informants, place, and date not given.

A Sponge Fishers' Charm, 1939, 123.
Greek. Reported by Eileen Elita Doering. Exact date and informants not given.

Ogres: Dracos and Baboulas, 1951, 307.
Greek. From a collection by Dorothy D. Lee of "traditional fears, told by Greeks of the Greater Boston area" who "had taken on American culture, in its externals, to a large degree." The informant, a mature woman, was from Lesbos. Name and date not given.

Omens of Death and Disaster, 1950, 392–93.
Japanese. Collected by Marvin K. Opler, Community Analyst, 1943–46, at the Segregation Center for Japanese, Tule Lake, California. He reports a revival of interest in Japanese folk beliefs and practices "as part of a total nativistic reaction" among the 25,000 internees at the Center from 1944 to 1946. Names of informants were not given.

Dreams, 1903, 134–35.
Syrian. Collected in Boston by Howard Barrett Wilson from natives of Syria. Exact date and names of informants not given.

Water Sleeps, 1935, 178.
Spanish-American. Collected by Helen Zunser from Fernán Lorenz of Hot Springs, northeastern New Mexico. Exact date not given.

Brujas in Texas, 1894, 142–44.
Spanish-American. Collected by Capt. John G. Bourke "during the time I was in command of the post of Fort Ringgold, Texas." His informant was Maria Antonia Cavazo de Garza, born in Rio Grande City, Texas, and between sixty-five and seventy in 1891 when Capt. Bourke first met her. She was reputed to be a *bruja*, or witch, but claimed to be merely a *curandera*, or healer.

Witches Outwitted, 1901, 39–40.
German-American. Collected by Elisabeth Cloud Seip in the summer of 1899 in Frederick County, Maryland, from informants of German descent. Exact place and names of informants not given.

Will-o'-the-wisp, 1888, 139.
American Negro. Collected by Alcée Fortier from French-speaking Negroes in Louisiana. Exact place, date, and names of informants not given. Compare "The Fire-Hunt," pp. 36–37.

Sign of a Hard Winter, 1902, 132.
Welsh-American. Collected by John L. Cowan of Allegheny, Pennsylvania, in a Pennsylvania mining town. The name of the town, informant, and date not given.

Signs and Countersigns, 1930, 325.
American Negro. Selected from a collection of Alabama material in the library of the Folklore Society of Hampton Institute by N. F. Woodall of Society Hill, Alabama. Date, place, and names of informants not given.

Halloween Projects, 1892, 318.
Anglo-American. Reported by Gertrude Decrow as current in Maine. Date, place, and informant not given. For a parallel, see *JAF* (1950), 315.

Cross-marks, 1899, 262.
American Negro. Collected by Roland Steiner, M.D., near Grovetown, Columbia County, central Georgia. Exact date and names of informants not given.

A Cross-mark to Relieve Distress, 1892, 230–31.
American Negro. Collected by Ruby Andrews Moore near Savannah, Georgia. Exact place, date, and name of informant not given.

Aches and Pains, 1899, 266–67.
    American Negro. Collected by Roland Steiner, M.D., near Grovetown, Georgia. Exact date and names of informants not given.

Warts, 1927, 170–71.
    Creole. Collected by Hilda Roberts in Iberia Parish, southwestern Louisiana, from white, Negro and Indian informants of French, Spanish and Anglo-Saxon descent. Exact date and further information not given.

Good Luck and Bad Luck, 1935, 329–30.
    Anglo-American. Collected by T. J. Farr "in the mountain and semi-mountain region of Tennessee." Exact date, place, and names of informants not given.

Spit and Sneeze, 1927, 164–65.
    Creole. Collected by Hilda Roberts in Iberia Parish, Louisiana, from white, Negro and Indian informants of French, Spanish and Anglo-Saxon descent. Exact date and further information about informants not given.

Pins and Needles, 1927, 181–82.
    Creole. Collected by Hilda Roberts in Iberia Parish, Louisiana, from white, Negro and Indian informants of French, Spanish and Anglo-Saxon descent. Exact date and further information about informants not given.

Beliefs about Marriage, 1918, 206–7.
    Anglo-American. Collected by Ethel Todd Norlin in the summer of 1915 at La Harpe, Hancock County, western Illinois, from middle-aged natives of English and Scottish descent. For further information about informants, see *JAF* (1918), 206–7.

Beliefs about Children, 1939, 112–13.
    Anglo-American. Collected by T. J. Farr in "the remote mountain sections" of Tennessee. The collection was "made over a period of several years" and includes "only those beliefs which have been reported to me by at least five different informants." No further information is given about informants, place, or date.

Hoodoo, 1927, 204–5.
    Creole. Collected by Hilda Roberts in Iberia Parish, Louisiana, from white, Negro and Indian informants of French, Spanish and Anglo-Saxon descent. Exact date and further information about informants not given.

Flyting with Witches, 1938, 47–50.
Anglo-American. Collected by S. P. Bayard from two "believers," Mary Pierson Rogers and Hannah Bayles Sayre. Mrs. Sayre's grandfather and her father, Aden Bayles, whose exploits she describes, were both "wizards" and "witch-doctors" who opposed practitioners of "evil magic." Aden Bayles was a farm laborer in Greene County, southwestern corner of Pennsylvania, and adjacent West Virginia. "Flyting" consists of scolding and cursing one's foe severely. See *JAF* (1938), 48, Footnote 1.

To Foil a Witch, 1935, 335.
Anglo-American. Collected by T. J. Farr "in the mountain and semi-mountain region of Tennessee." Exact date, place, and names of informants not given.

Plants, Birds, Animals and Insects, 1950, 318–23.
Anglo-American. Collected by Lelah Allison "in the Wabash region in southeastern Illinois," a region settled by the English and former residents of southern states who were of English descent.

Nudity and Planting Customs, 1953, 333–34.
Anglo-American. Reported by Vance Randolph who provides references to similar vegetation rites and related folk customs in his footnotes but no further information about informants.

PROVERBS

Yiddish Proverbs, 1920, 136–38, 144–48.
Russian-Jewish. Collected by Leah Rachel Yoffie in St. Louis, Missouri, from "immigrants who have lived in the city for twenty-five years or more." The collection was completed prior to October 1919.

Coplas from New Mexico, 1913, 111–15.
Spanish-American. Collected by Aurelio M. Espinosa "in Albuquerque and Santa Fe, from less than a half-dozen persons." *Coplas* are couplets, often of a satirical or proverbial nature. They are sung to standard tunes. Translation by Patricia Del Rio.

Proverbs from Massachusetts, 1906, 122.
Anglo-American. Reported from rural Massachusetts by Helen M. Thurston. Exact place, date and informants not given.

A Proverbial Rhyme, 1951, 318.
 Anglo-American. Collected by Herbert Halpert from Mary
 Clayton Long of Marshall County, Tennessee. Exact date not
 given. It closely parallels rhymes recorded in Lancashire, England, and Scotland. See *JAF* (1951), 317–19.

Gullah Proverbs, 1925, 228–29.
 American Negro. Collected in 1923 from children of Penn
 School, St. Helena's Island, South Carolina. "Gullah" or
 "Geechee" is a dialect spoken by Negroes of coastal South
 Carolina and Georgia.

Geechee Proverbs, 1919, 442.
 American Negro. Compiled by Monroe N. Work from a collection published in the *Southern Workman,* November
 1905. See note above.

RIDDLES

Polish Riddles, 1949, 189.
 Polish. Collected on June 19, 1946, in Crystal Falls, Michigan,
 by Archer Taylor, who supplies references to Polish parallels.
 Names of informants not given.

Lithuanian Riddles, 1950, 325–27.
 Lithuanian. Collected in 1949 by Jonas Balys from Ursula
 Žemaitis, a native of Lankeliškiai parish, southwest Lithuania,
 who was born in 1890 and came to the United States in 1914.
 In 1949 she was employed as a charwoman. Presented here
 are "such riddles as are not very often heard among Lithua-
 nians of today."

Syrian Riddles, 1903, 135–36.
 Syrian. Collected by Howard Barrett Wilson from natives of
 Syria living in Boston. Exact date and names of informants
 not given.

Mexican Riddles, 1938, 83.
 Mexican. Collected in New York City by Carlota Garfias in
 December 1936; the first riddle from María Garfias of Mulegé,
 Lower California, and the second from V. R. Garfias of Mex-
 ico City.

Pennsylvania Dutch Riddles, 1906, 113–17.
 Pennsylvania Dutch. Collected by Jonathan Baer Stoudt of
 Lancaster, Pennsylvania. Exact date and informants not given.

A Connecticut Riddle Tale, 1935, 197.
Anglo-American or American Negro. Collected by Mrs. E. M.
Backus in rural Connecticut in the late nineteenth century.
Date, place, and informant not given. For other riddle tales
see *JAF* (1934), 77, and (1954), 253. For a similar riddle
detached from the tale, see *JAF* (1925), 228.

Riddles from South Carolina, 1922, 326–27.
American Negro. Collected in 1894 by Miss A. M. Bacon from
J. W. Bedenbaugh of Bradley, South Carolina, then a student
at Hampton Institute. Parallels to other riddles in *JAF* and in
Elsie Clews Parsons, *Folk-Lore of the Sea Islands, South
Carolina*, Publications of the American Folklore Society,
Memoir xvi (Philadelphia, 1923), are cited in Miss Bacon's
footnotes.

Riddles from South Carolina, with Variants, 1921, 24–29.
American Negro. Collected by Elsie Clews Parsons in March
1920 from Negro children in the Aiken, South Carolina,
public school. For parallels see Miss Parsons' footnotes.

Riddles from Louisiana, 1922, 106–7.
American Negro. Collected by A. E. Perkins in March 1920
from Negro school children in New Orleans whose parents
were English-speaking and born in Mississippi.

Riddles from New Jersey, 1943, 200–1.
American Negro. Collected by Herbert Halpert in South
Tom's River, New Jersey, in June 1941 from Louvira Brannen,
age sixty-eight, who was born about fifty-five miles from Savannah, Georgia. These riddles should be compared with
other American riddles presented here.

Ozark Mountain Riddles, 1934, 82–83.
Anglo-American. Collected by Vance Randolph and Isabel
Spradley from unnamed informants in McDonald, Barry,
Stone and Taney counties of southwestern Missouri and Ben-
ton, Carroll, Boone and Washington counties in Arkansas.
Exact date not given.

A Blue Ridge Mountain Riddle, 1934, 76.
Anglo-American. Collected by Isabel Gordon Carter during
the summer of 1923 from Jane Gentry, of Hot Springs, North
Carolina, then more than sixty years old. She stated that in
her "mother's day they used to tell riddles all night long and
the best riddle got a prize, but in my day they sang all night
long and the best song got a prize."

Riddles from Tennessee, 1935, 318–19.
Anglo-American. Collected by T. J. Farr "in the mountain

and semi-mountain region of Tennessee." Exact date, place, and names of informants not given.

Riddles from Arkansas, 1954, 255–59.
Anglo-American. Collected by Vance Randolph and Mary Celestia Parler between 1944 and 1953 from Arkansas natives. For complete information on informants, see *JAF* (1954), 253–59.

GAMES

Woskate Takapsice or Sioux Shinney, 1905, 283–85.
American Indian. Observed and reported by J. R. Walker as played by the Dakota Sioux.

The King's Army, 1907, 248.
Anglo-American. Reported by Haywood Parker as peculiar to the southern Appalachian Mountains of North Carolina. Exact place and date not given. Compare "London Bridge Is Falling Down."

A Game with Eggs on Easter, 1903, 138–39.
Syrian. Described by Howard Barrett Wilson as current among natives of Syria living in Boston. The same custom has been recorded from the Armenians in *JAF* (1899), 107, and observed in Lexington County, South Carolina, among descendants of Palatine Germans who settled this region in the 1730s.

A Counting Game, 1892, 15–16.
Portuguese Azores. Collected by Henry R. Lang from natives of the Azores, especially the island of Fayal, living in New Bedford, Massachusetts. Date and informant not given.

A Rapid Counting Contest, 1938, 84.
Mexican. Collected in New York City from María Gorosave of Lower California in December 1936 by Carlota Garfias.

A Mexican Ring Game, 1938, 85.
Mexican. Collected in New York City from Isabel Pierro of Chiapas, Mexico, in December 1936 by Carlota Garfias.

The Little Coyote, 1916, 513–14.
Spanish-American. Collected in New Mexico by Aurelio M. Espinosa. These games are similar to *Los Pollitos* ["The Chickens"—colloquially, boys or girls], from Extremadura, Spain. The *coyotito* in the New Mexican game takes the place

of the *lobito* or "little wolf" of the Spanish game. The second
part of the game, the capture of the *pollitos* by the *lobito*,
and paying a ransom to get them back is not known in the
New Mexican version.

A Guessing Game with Pecans, 1888, 139.
Louisiana French. Reported as current by Alcée Fortier.

Club Fist, 1943, 204.
American Indian. Collected by Mary K. Rowell from Mrs.
G. M. Cook, age seventy-eight, a Pamunkey Indian. Mem-
bers of this tribe live in the Rappahannock area of Virginia.
Other games played by the Pamunkey Indians suggesting
English influence include "Spin the Plate," "Blind Man's
Buff," and "Hide the Switch."

Ring Games of Negro Children, 1917, 218–20.
American Negro. Collected by Loraine Darby from Negro
children in southern Georgia. Exact date and place not given.

Quebec Town, 1892, 118.
Anglo-American. Reported by N. C. Hoke of Lincolnton,
North Carolina, as current in a neighborhood whose original
settlers "were almost exclusively Germans." The seated player
is presumably mourning the absence of a lover who is in the
army.

An Evening Party Song-Game, 1901, 295–96.
Anglo-American. Emma M. Backus stated: "These games I
saw played in the towns of Ashford and Eastford [Connecti-
cut] in the year 1865. The music was procured from Mrs.
Charles Perrin, who played the games in her youth."

Snap, 1936, 199.
Anglo-American. Reported by Vance Randolph and Nancy
Clemens. Exact place and date not given but well known in
Oklahoma and Missouri in the late nineteenth century and
thereafter.

A Ball-Bouncing Game, 1947, 30.
Anglo-American. Collected from children on the St. Louis,
Missouri, playgrounds in 1944 by Leah Rachel Yoffie, this
game rhyme has been frequently recorded in England and
North America. See *JAF* (1947), 31, Footnote 122.

A Ball-Bouncing and Rope-Jumping Song, 1947, 46.
Anglo-American. Collected by Leah Rachel Yoffie in St. Louis
in 1944; not found in her survey made in 1914.

Jump-Rope Rhymes, 1945, 349–51.
Anglo-American. Collected by Herbert Halpert from game

rhymes of girls, ages nine to twelve, of Manchester, New Hampshire, published in the *Manchester Leader* in the summer of 1945. See Lucy Nulton, "Jump Rope Rhymes as Folk Literature," *JAF* (1948), 53–67.

A Political Jump-Rope Rhyme, 1963, 133.
Anglo-American. Collected by Martin Light on November 30, 1960, shortly after the presidential campaign, from a child in the first grade of the Burtsfield School in West Lafayette, Indiana. See the note in *JAF* (1963), 133.

Counting Out Rhymes, with Variants, 1918, 522–23.
Anglo-American. Collected in 1914–15 from students at Michigan State Normal College, all of whom were Michigan natives, by Emelyn E. Gardner. For references to other versions of these rhymes, see *JAF* (1918), 522–23.

A Children's Dance Rhyme, 1899, 293–94.
Anglo-American. Collected by May Ovington from Brooklyn, New York, children. Exact date not given. In the English game of "Milking Pails" a mother is confronted by a row of daughters who sing:

> Mary's gone a-milking,
> Mother, mother;
> Mary's gone a-milking,
> Gentle, sweet mother of mine.

The mother tells the daughters, "Take your pails and follow," but the daughters ask her to "buy me a pair of new milking pails." The mother asks: "Where's the money to come from?" and the daughters reply that they can sell the father's feather bed. The game ends with the pursuit and punishment of the wicked children. See note by W. W. Newell in *JAF* (1899), 294.

Hop Scotch, 1891, 229.
Anglo-American. One of several street games collected by Stewart Culin from "a lad of ten years residing in Brooklyn, New York, as games in which he himself had taken part." Exact date is not given.

FOLK DRAMA AND FOLK FESTIVAL

A Miracle Play of the Rio Grande, 1893, 90–95.
Spanish-American. John G. Bourke, who describes this Nativity play, states that it is typical of such performances from

the "Lower Rio Grande" valley of Texas and Mexico. For a complete text see M. R. Cole, *Los Pastores: A Mexican Play of the Nativity,* Publications of the American Folklore Society, Memoir IX (Philadelphia, 1907).

Christmas Masking in Boston, 1896, 178.
Anglo-American. Collected by W. W. Newell from John A. Fulton of Cambridge, Massachusetts, who "belonged to a family identified with colonial Massachusetts."

A Mummers' Play from the Kentucky Mountains, 1938, 10–15.
Anglo-American. Collected by Marie Campbell for whom it was presented "on Christmas Eve in 1930" by "some of the men and boys at Gander." After the performance she obtained "a fairly complete text" from two of the actors, Tom and George Fields. "Thirty or more years had passed since its last performance."

Seeking Jesus, 1901, 172.
American Negro. Recorded by Roland Steiner, M.D., near Grovetown, Georgia. Exact date not given.

Mother, Mother, the Milk's Boiling Over, 1927, 38–39.
Anglo-American. Collected by Jean Olive Heck, ca. 1906, from elementary school children, Fifth District, Cincinnati, Ohio. Exact date and names of informants not given.

A Ring Game from North Carolina, 1921, 113.
American Negro. Collected in Raleigh, North Carolina, by Susan Dix Spenney. Exact date not given.

A Slovak Harvest Festival in New Jersey, 1956, 272–73, 275–76.
Slovakian. Described by Svatava Pirkova-Jakobson. The participants were natives of Vrbovce, a Slovak mountain village on the Moravian border, and their families, residing at Heightstown, New Jersey. The festival and play took place in the fall, about three years prior to the publication of the description. For details on Vrbovce where "the traditional life of the village has not changed," and generalization on the significance of the festival for the participants, see *JAF* (1956), 274–75.

A Corpus Christi Festival in Pennsylvania, 1898, 126–28.
German. Described by Charles Burr Todd. The festival took place at St. Mary's, Pennsylvania, in the heart of the Appalachian chain, a village founded in the 1840s as a Catholic community and settled by Catholics from Alsace, Bavaria, and Belgium.

The *Penitentes* of New Mexico, 1963, 220–21.
> Spanish-American. Described by Juan Hernandez as typical of the observances of the *Penitente* brotherhoods "in the isolated mountain villages of northeastern New Mexico."

A Lenten Procession in Arizona, 1957, 140–41.
> American Indian. Described by George C. Barker. His "personal impressions of the nocturnal procession of the sixth Friday in Lent at Pascua village on the outskirts of Tucson, Arizona, were recorded in April 1955." Pascua is a Yaqui Indian village. For an interpretation of the Pascua procession and a comparison with Penitential processions in Spain and the American Southwest, see *JAF* (1957), 137–42.

INDEX

ETHNIC GROUPS AND LOCALITIES

Adjectives (e.g. "Anglo-American") designate material from immigrant and native groups in North America (including Canada and Mexico); noun references are to place names in the text or to material originating in them.

Africa, Kamerum, 3, 228
Alabama, 114–15, 237
Alsatian, 14–15, 75, 217–20, 229, 245
Amish, 75–77, 234
Anglo-American, 28–29, 29–32, 32–33, 36–37, 37–38, 38–41, 41–42, 49–50, 61–62, 68–69, 70–71, 71, 78–80, 85–87, 87, 90–92, 99, 115–16, 120–22, 124–26, 126–28, 131–33, 133, 134–37, 137–39, 149, 160, 165–66, 167, 167–69, 169–70, 176, 184, 184–86, 186–87, 187–88, 188–89, 189, 190–91, 191–92, 192–93, 204–5, 205–11, 212–13, 230, 231, 232, 233, 234, 235, 236, 237, 238, 239, 240, 241, 242, 243, 244, 245. See also England
Arizona, Tucson, 224–25, 246
Arkansas, 165–66, 169–70, 241, 242
Armenian, Harpoot, 5, 228
Army, U. S., 43–44, 231
Azores, Fayal, 177–78, 242

Belgian, 217–20, 245

California: Berkeley, 3, 228; Camp Stoneman, 43–44, 231; Los Angeles, 44, 63, 231, 233; Oakland, 3, 99, 228, 236; Tule Lake, 106–7, 236
Canada, 14–15, 228, 229; New Brunswick, 29; Nova Scotia, Lequille, 23–25, 229; Quebec, Cédres, 53–55, 232, Lorette, 9–11, 228, Montreal, 53–55, 232, Quebec, 184
Cape Verde, 56–60, 232
Chinese: Manchurian, 7–9, 228; Shantung Province, 7–9
Colorado, 5; Denver, 235
Connecticut, 160, 241; Ashford, 184–86, 243; Eastford, 184–86, 243
Cornish-American, 44–46, 232
Creole, 119–20, 122–23, 123–24, 128–31, 238

Denmark, Laaland, 14, 229

Dutch-American, 19–23, 55, 229, 232. *See also* Pennsylvania Dutch

England, 13–14, 37–38, 124–26, 134–37, 187, 191–92, 238, 239, 243, 244; Lancashire, 149, 240

Finnish, 103–5, 236; Kangasniemi, 104; Oulu, 103
Florida, Tarpon Springs, 105
France, 15–17
French Canadian, 9–11, 53–55, 228, 232

Georgia, 17–19, 181–83, 229, 243; Grovetown, 72–74, 116–17, 117, 211, 234, 237, 238, 245; Savannah, 117, 165, 237, 241
German and German-American, 14–15, 75, 111–13, 177, 217–20, 229, 237, 242, 243, 245
Greek, 11–12, 105, 105–6, 228, 236; Lesbos, 105–6, 236

Hawaii, 95–98, 235; Honolulu, 96–97

Illinois: Chicago, 88–89, 235; East St. Louis, 26–28, 230; Egypt, 15–17, 32, 229; Grand Tower, 15–17, 229; Jonesboro, 32, 230; La Harpe, 124–26, 238; Thebes, 32, 230; Wabash, 134–37, 239
Indian (American), 173–75, 180–81, 224–25; Cherokee, 139; Isleta Pueblo, 4–5, 228; Micmac, 23–25, 229; Pamunkey, 180–81, 243;

Ponka, 51; Pseudo-, 93–94, 235; Sioux, 51–52, 173–75, 232, 242; Yaqui, 224–25, 246
Indiana: Goshen, 75–77, 234; West Lafayette, 189, 244
Irish and Irish-American, 14, 15–17, 23–25, 229
Iowa, 41, 76; Elkader, 41–42, 231; Little Switzerland, 41–42, 231

Japanese, 3, 106–7, 228, 236
Jewish, 44, 142–45, 231, 239

Kansas, Sidney, 68–69, 233
Kentucky, 29–32, 137, 205–11, 230, 245

Lithuanian, 154–55, 240; Lankeliškiai, 154–55, 240
Louisiana, 92, 113, 180, 237, 243; Iberia Parish, 119–20, 122–23, 123–24, 128–31, 238; New Orleans, 164, 241; Violet, 34, 230

Maine, 115–16, 237; Brunswick, 28–29, 230
Maryland, Frederick County, 111–13, 237
Massachusetts, 56–60, 149, 232, 239; Boston, 11–12, 105–6, 107–9, 204–5, 228, 236, 240, 242, 245; Cambridge, 68–69, 204–5, 233, 245; New Bedford, 177–78, 242
Mexico, 63, 178–79, 179, 197–204, 233, 240, 242, 245; Chiapas, 179, 242; Chihuahua, 81, 83; Lower California, 157, 178–79, 179, 240, 242; Mexico City,

Mexico (*cont'd*)
  157, 240; Parras, 110. *See also* Spanish-American
Michigan, 85–87, 190–91, 234, 244; Crystal Falls, 154, 240; Detroit, 5, 228; Ishpeming, 44–46, 232; Whitehall, 70–71, 233
Minnesota, 14, 103–5, 229, 236; Crooked Lake, 103; Winton, 104
Mississippi: Oxford, 71, 87, 233, 235; Rena Lara, 87, 235
Missouri, 138–39, 165–66, 186–87, 241, 243; Aurora, 138; Joplin, 137; MacDonald County, 138; St. Louis, 26–28, 142–45, 187, 188, 239, 243
Mormon, 88, 235

Negro: African (Bulu), 3, 228; American, 17–19, 26–28, 41–42, 72–74, 74–75, 88–89, 113, 114–15, 116–17, 117, 117–18, 150, 150–51, 160, 160–61, 161–63, 164, 165, 181–83, 211, 213–14, 229, 230, 231, 234, 235, 237, 238, 240, 241, 243, 245; Louisiana French, 113, 180, 237, 243; Micmac, 23–25, 229; Portuguese, 56–60, 232
New Hampshire, Manchester, 188–89, 244
New Jersey: Chatsworth, 37; Heightstown, 214–17, 245; New Egypt, 37–38, 231; South Tom's River, 165, 241; Trenton, 215
New Mexico, 5, 145–49, 179–80, 220–23, 242, 246; Albuquerque, 145–49, 239;

Hot Springs, 25, 109, 229, 237; Santa Fé, 145–49, 239
New York, 41–42; Brooklyn, 191–92, 192–93, 244; Buffalo, 90; New York City, 157, 178–79, 179, 216, 240, 242; Old Hurley, 55, 232
North Carolina, 41–42, 176, 231, 242; Cumberland, 36; Fayetteville, 36; Fisher's River, 36–37; Fletcher, 33, 230; Hot Springs, 167, 241; Lincolntown, 184, 243; Raleigh, 213–14, 245
North Dakota, 14
Norway, 64
Norwegian-American, 64–67, 233

Ohio: Bellaire, 131; Cincinnati, 212–13, 245
Oklahoma, 139, 186–87, 243

Pennsylvania, 75, 131–33, 239; Allegheny, 113–14, 237; Harrisburg, 61–62, 233; Lancaster, 157–59, 240; Philadelphia, 41–42, 231; St. Mary's, 217–20, 245
Pennsylvania Dutch, 157–59, 240
Polish, 154, 240
Puerto Rican, 34–36, 230

Rhode Island, 56–60, 232
Russian, 142–45, 239

Scottish, 12–13, 38–41, 124–26, 149, 228, 238, 240
Slovakian, 214–17, 245
South Carolina, 211; Aiken, 161–63, 241; Bradley, 160–61, 241; Lexington County,

South Carolina (cont'd)
177, 242; St. Helena's Island, 150, 240
Spain, 222, 224–25, 246; Extremadura, 179–80, 242
Spanish-American, 25, 34, 63, 81–85, 109, 109–11, 145–49, 179–80, 197–204, 220–23, 229, 230, 233, 234, 237, 239, 242, 244, 246. See also Spain
Syrian, 107–9, 156, 177, 236, 240, 242; B'shory, 109

Tennessee, 120–22, 126–28, 133, 137, 167–69, 238, 239,

241; Cade's Cove, 49–50, 232; Elkmont, 12–14, 229; Marshall County, 149, 240
Texas, 197–204, 245; Beeville, 74–75, 234; Brownsville, 81–85, 234; Rio Grande City, 109–11, 237

Utah, 88, 235; Clearfield, 93–94, 235

Virginia, 137, 180–81, 243; Huntly, 90–92, 235

Welsh-American, 113–14, 237
West Virginia, 131–33, 239

COLLECTORS, INFORMANTS, AND TRANSLATORS

Allison, Lelah, 134–37, 239
Ashheim, Julian, 81–85, 234

Backus, Emma M., 17–19, 72–74, 160, 184–86, 229, 234, 241, 243
Bacon, A. M., 160–61, 241
Balys, Jonas, 154–55, 240
Barbeau, C.-Marius, 9–11, 53–55, 228, 232
Barker, George C., 224–25, 246
Barry, Phillips, 61–62, 68–69, 233
Bayard, Samuel P., 131–33, 239
Bayles, Aden, 131–33, 239
Beck, Horace P., 90–92, 235
Bedenbaugh, J. W., 160–61, 241
Bernardi, Herschel, 44, 232
Beverley, William H., 43–44, 231
Boggs, Ralph, 36–37, 231

Bourke, John G., 109–11, 197–204, 237, 244
Brannen, Louvina, 165, 241
Briegel, George F., 88, 235
Broadhead, Mrs. Grispell, 55, 232
Brunette, Mrs. G. A., 87, 235
Burnette, A. H., 87, 235

C., O.F.A., 61–62, 233
C., T.P., 9–11, 34–36, 53–55, 228, 230, 232
Campbell, Marie, 205–11, 245
Canada, Floyd, 74–75, 234
Carter, Isabel G., 12–14, 167, 228, 241
Cavazo de Garcia, Maria A., 109–11, 237
Černek, Sam, 216
Christensen, Julian, 14, 229
Clark, June, 29–32, 230
Claudel, Calvin, 34, 230
Clemens, Nancy, 186–87, 243
Cole, Helen R., 41–42, 231
Collazo, Francisco, 199

Cook, Mrs. G. M., 180–81, 243
Corella, Carlotta M., 63, 233
Cowan, John L., 113–14, 237
Cox, J. Harrington, 26–28, 230
Cray, Ed, 44, 231
Culin, Stewart, 192–93, 244

Darby, Loraine, 181–83, 243
Davidson, Levette J., 88, 235
Decrow, Gertrude, 115–16, 237
Del Rio, Patricia, 145–49, 239
Dobie, J. Frank, 81–85, 234
Doering, Eileen E., 105, 236
Dorsey, J. Owen, 51–52, 232
Dorsey, Thomas A., 235
Dorson, Richard M., 44–46, 232

Edgar, Marjorie, 103–5, 236
Espinosa, Aurelio M., 4–5, 34–36, 145–49, 179–80, 228, 239, 242

Farr, T. J., 120–22, 126–28, 133, 167–69, 238, 239, 241
Fauset, Arthur H., 23–25, 41–42, 229, 231
Fields, George, 205–11, 245
Fields, Tom, 205–11, 245
Fife, Austin, 93–94, 235
Fortier, Alcée, 113, 180, 237, 243
Freeman, Linton C., 95–98, 235
Freisen, John, 75–77, 234
Fulton, John A., 204–5, 245

Gardner, Emelyn E., 5, 70–71, 190–91, 228, 233, 244
Garfias, Carlota, 157, 178–79, 179, 240–42
Garfias, María, 157, 240
Garfias, V. R., 157
Gay, Edwin F., 85–87, 234

Gentry, Jane, 167, 241
Gorosave, María, 178–79, 242
Gould, C. N., 14, 229
Gracey, Louis, 99, 236
Grant, Charles H., 37–38, 231
Green, Archie, 99, 235
Gries, Walter F., 44–46, 232

Hague, Eleanor, 63, 233
Halpert, Herbert, 37–38, 149, 165, 188–89, 231, 240, 241, 243
Harmon, Mrs. Samuel, 49–50, 232
Harris, Harriett C., 19–23
Harris, Henrietta C., 19–23
Haugen, Einar, 64–67, 233
Heck, Jean O., 212–13, 245
Henry, Mrs. Mellinger, 49–50, 232
Hernandez, Juan, 220–23, 246
Hill, A. Lulu, 26–28, 230
Hoke, N. C., 184, 243
Hoogasian, Susie, 5, 228
Hsü Tsan Hwa, 7–8, 228
Hudson, Arthur P., 87, 235

I., N., 3, 228
Ives, Edward D., 28–29, 230

La Flèche, Francis, 51–52, 232
Lang, Henry R., 177–78, 242
Larin, Joseph, 53–55, 232
Lauridson, Cora B., 93–94
Leach, MacEdward, 90–92, 235
Lee, Buck, 93–94, 235
Lee, Dorothy D., 11–12, 105–6, 228, 236
Legault, Alfred, 53–55, 232
Light, Martin, 189, 244
Lomax, John, 85–87, 234
Long, Mary C., 149, 240

Longini, Muriel D., 88–89, 235
Lorenz, Antonio, 25, 229
Lorenz, Fernán, 109, 237

Margrave, Wendell, 32, 230
Mason, J. Alden, 34–36, 230
Massicote, E.-Z., 53–55, 232
Moore, Ruby A., 117, 237

Neely, Charles, 15–17, 229
Nekarda, Anna, 215
Neuhaus, John, 99, 236
Newell, William W., 78–80, 204–5, 234, 245
Norlin, Ethel T., 124–26, 238

Opler, Marvin K., 106–7, 236
Ovington, May, 191–92, 244

Paredes, Américo, 81–85
Parker, Haywood, 176, 242
Parker, (Mr.), 41–42, 231
Parler, Mary C., 169–70, 242
Parsons, Elsie C., 56–60, 161–63, 232, 241
Pendleton, Silas, 90–92, 235
Pennall, Joe, 23–25, 229
Pennall, Peter, 23–25
Perkins, A. E., 164, 241
Perrin, Mrs. Charles, 184–86
Perrin, James, 41–42, 231, 243
Perrow, E. C., 71, 233
Pierro, Isabel, 179, 242
Pirkova-Jakobsen, Svatava, 214–17, 245
Porter, Kenneth W., 38–41, 231

Randolph, Vance, 137–39, 165–66, 169–70, 186–87, 239, 241, 242, 243
Rankin, J. E., 71, 233
Redden, Francesca, 93–94, 235

Richard, A., 28–29, 230
Ring, Constance V., 55, 232
Roberts, Helen H., 56–60, 232
Roberts, Hilda, 119–20, 122–23, 123–24, 128–31, 238
Rogers, Mary P., 131–33, 239
Rowell, Mary K., 180–81, 243

S., M.A., 68–69, 233
Sapir, Edward, 7–8, 228
Sartalamacchia, Katherine, 34, 230
Sayre, Hannah B., 131–33, 239
Schumaker, Frank, 15–17, 229
Schwab, George, 3, 228
Seip, Elisabeth C., 111–13, 237
Sioui, Clément, 9–11, 228
Sioui, P., 9–11, 228
Smith, Grace P., 32, 230
Spenney, Susan D., 213–14, 245
Spradley, Isabel, 165–66, 241
Srabian, Mary, 5, 228
Steiner, Roland, 116–17, 117, 211, 237, 238, 245
Stoudt, Jonathan B., 157–59, 240
Stroup, Thomas B., 33, 230

Taliaferro, Harden E., 36–37, 231
Taylor, Archer, 14–15, 229, 240
Thurston, Helen M., 149, 239
Todd, Charles B., 217–20, 245

Umble, John, 75–77, 234

W., H.L., 68–69, 233
Walker, J. R., 173–75
Webb, Walter P., 74–75, 234
Wilkinson, Susie, 12–14, 228

Wilson, Howard B., 107–9, 156, 177, 236, 240, 242

Wintemberg, W. M., 14–15, 229

Woodall, N. F., 114–15, 237

Work, Monroe N., 150–51, 240

Yates, Norris, 43–44, 231

Yoder, Don, 75–77, 234

Yoffie, Leah R., 142–45, 187–88, 239, 243

Youngquist, Livia, 70–71, 233

Zemaitas, Ursala, 154–55, 240

Zunser, Helen, 25, 109, 229, 237

TITLES AND FIRST LINES OF SONGS

AIN'T GWINE GRIEVE MY GOD NO MORE, 72–74

Asesinato de Francisco Villa, 81–85

Aunt Jane had a dance and she had a crowd, 88–89

Before time at night you could go out, 96

Before time when you go to town, 97

Benedito seja Deus para sempre, 56–60

BISHOP ZACK, 88

Body surfing at Makapuu, 96

Bring me a note from the dungeons deep, 37

C'est dans Paris; savez-vous c(e) qu'il y a?, 53–55

THE DEATH OF THE BECKWITH CHILD, 78–80

THE DEHORN SONG, 99

The dehorn's nose is deepest red, 99

Did you go to the henhouse? 181–82

Duke Kahanamoku, the champion of Oahu, 98

Every time you hear me sing this song, 74–75

Fort Street mauka, now makai, 97

Granddaddy is dead and laid in his grave, 214

THE HAUNTED WOOD, 93–94

Hypocrite, hypocritè, God despise, 72–74

I served with old Bob Lee three years about, 87

I was on the Drive in eighty, 85–87

I went down town to buy a car, 97

I'M A GOOD OLD REBEL, 87
AN INDIAN LOVE SONG, 51–52
I'VE A LONG TIME HEARD, 71
I've a long time heard the sun will be bleeding, 71

La Estrella del Norte, 63
Lester Petrie, he runs the town, 98
Lob-Gesang, 75–77

McKinley went to Buffalo, thought he knew it all, 90–92
The marines landed in Kailua Bay, 97
Men skulde du deg som andre Klare, 64–67
THE MUMMERS' CAROL, 211
My frends allow my febel tongue, 78–80

Neste dia do Janer, 56–60

THE OCEAN BURIAL, 61–62
O Gott Vater wir loben Dich, 75–77
Oh, bury me not in the deep, deep seal, 61–62
Oh! my true love, she was handsome, 68–69
Oh Huey Long was a good old man, 90–92
On the banks there lived a white man, 93–94

PIG IN THE PARLOR, 70–71

RAILROAD BLUES, 74–75
La Randonnée de la Ville de Paris, 53–55

Sailing in the boat when the tide runs high, 184–86
San José Sagrada da Maria Angelina, 56–60
SELLIN' THAT STUFF, 88–89
SILVER JACK, 85–87
SONGS FOR CHRISTMAS AND THE NEW YEAR, 56–60

TEN THOUSAND MILES AWAY, 68–69
There is six days all in a week, 211
Took my girl for a buggy ride, 97
Trippa, Troppa, Tronjes, 55
Trippa, Troppa, Tronjes! De varkens in de boonjes, 55
THE TWO SISTERS, 49–50

U.S.E.D. Suckers every day, 95–98
THE UNQUIET GRAVE, 37

Vemé, vemé con esos tus ojos, 63

Villa, doquiera que te halles, 81–85

Was two sisters loved one man, 49–50
Way down yonder, soup to soup, 183
We are marching down to Quebec town, 184
We've got a new pig in the parlor, 70–71
When I think of you, I am weeping as I go!, 51–52

You vote for mayor Crane, 98
You vote for Tommy Lee, 98

Zack Black came to Utah back in Eighty-three, 88

TALE TYPES

References here are to the tale types established by Antti Aarne and Stith Thompson in *The Types of the Folk-Tale*, Helsinki, 1928.

301: The Three Stolen Princesses, 5
313A: The Girl as Helper, 19–23
330B: The Devil in the Knapsack (Bottle, Cask), 15–17
465: The Man Persecuted Because of his Beautiful Wife, 15–17
766: The Seven Sleepers, 34
780: The Singing Bone, 49–50
882: The Wager on the Wife's Chastity, 11–12
921: The King and the Peasant's Son, 12–14
1060–1114: Contest between Man and Ogre, 23–25
1419H: Woman Warns Lover of Husband by Singing Song, 11–12
1525M: Mak and the Sheep, 33
1533: The Wise Carving of the Fowl, 14
1561: The Lazy Boy Eats Breakfast, Dinner, and Supper One after the Other, 25
1700: "I don't Know", 34–36
1839: The Card-playing Parson, 44
1890E: Gun Barrel Bent, 43–44

MOTIFS

References to typology of Stith Thompson, *Motif-Index of Folk-Literature*, 6 vols., Bloomington, Indiana University Press, 1955–58.

A 1650.1 — The various children of Eve, 4–5

D 1531.7 — Witch flies with aid of magic juice, 15

D 1960.1 — Seven sleepers, 34

F 54.2 — Plant grows to sky, 30

F 262 f. — Fairies make music, 24

F 491.1 — Will-o'-the-Wisp leads people astray, 36–37

G 224.2 — Witch's salve, 15

G 241.1.6 — Witch rides on cattle, 15

G 242.1.1 — Witch smears fat on brooms in preparation for flight, 15

G 242.7 — Person flying with witches makes mistake and falls, 15

G 303 — Devil, 23–25

G 440 — Ogre abducts person, 42

H 561.5 — King and clever minister, 12–14

H 583.3 — King: What is your brother doing? Youth: He hunts; he throws away what he catches and what he does not catch he carries with him, 13

H 583.5 — King: What is your sister doing? Youth: She is mourning last year's laughter, 13

H 603 — Symbolic interpretation of playing cards, 9–11

H 1023.2 — Task: carrying water in a sieve, 3

H 1054.3 f. — Task: coming neither naked nor clad, 12

J 1189 — Clever means of avoiding legal punishment, 12–14

J 1495.2 — When Caleb comes, 26–28

J 1510 f. — The cheater cheated, 3

J 1730 f. — Absurd ignorance, 32

J 1930 f. — Absurd disregard of natural laws, 32

J 2496.2 — Misunderstandings because of lack of knowledge of a different language than one's own, 34–36

K 10-100 — Contests won by deception, 23–25

K 621 — Escape by blinding the guard, 18

K 842.1 — Dupe persuaded to take prisoner's place suspended in air, 18–19

K 1600 f. — Deceiver falls into own trap, 3

L 50 — Victorious youngest daughter, 8

M 210 — Bargain with devil, 23–25

Q 451.10 — Punishment: genitalia cut off, 38

R 11 — Abduction by monster, 42

S 31 — Cruel stepmother, 7–8

W 152 f. — Stinginess, 38–41

X 1130.2 f. — Fruit tree grows from head of deer shot with fruit pits, 30

X 1132.1 — The nailed wolf's tail, 32

X 1761 — Absurd disregard of the nature of holes, 32